PENGUIN PLAYS

EARLY DAYS, SISTERS
AND LIFE CLASS

David Storey was born in 1933 and is the third son of a
mine-worker. He was educated at the Queen Elizabeth
Grammar School in Wakefield and the Slade School of
Fine Art. He has had various jobs ranging from professional footballer to school-teacher and showground tent-
erector. He is now both a novelist and a dramatist.

Among his publications are *This Sporting Life*, which
won the Macmillan Fiction Award in 1960 and was also
filmed; *Flight into Camden*, which won the John Llewelyn
Rhys Memorial Prize and the Somerset Maugham Award
in 1960; *Radcliffe*, and *Pasmore*, which won the Faber
Memorial Prize in 1973. These were followed by *A
Temporary Life*, *Edward*, and *Saville*, which won the
Booker Prize in 1976. His other plays include *In Cele-
bration*, which has been filmed, *Home*, *The Contractor*
and *The Changing Room*. Many of these are published in
Penguin.

David Storey lives in London. He was married in 1956
and has four children.

EARLY DAYS
SISTERS
AND
LIFE CLASS

*

DAVID STOREY

PENGUIN BOOKS

Penguin Books Ltd, Harmondsworth, Middlesex, England
Penguin Books, 625 Madison Avenue, New York, New York 10022, U.S.A.
Penguin Books Australia Ltd, Ringwood, Victoria, Australia
Penguin Books Canada Ltd, 2801 John Street, Markham, Ontario, Canada L3R 1B4
Penguin Books (N.Z.) Ltd, 182–190 Wairau Road, Auckland 10, New Zealand

—

Life Class first published by Jonathan Cape 1975
Copyright © David Storey, 1975
Early Days and *Sisters* first published by Penguin Books 1980
Copyright © David Storey, 1980
This edition published in Penguin Books 1980
All rights reserved

—

All inquiries regarding amateur rights in *Life Class* to be
addressed to Samuel French Ltd, 26 Southampton Street,
London WC2.
All inquiries regarding professional productions of the
plays and amateur rights in *Sisters* and *Early Days* to be
addressed to Fraser and Dunlop (Scripts) Ltd, 91 Regent
Street, London W1.

—

Filmset, printed and bound in Great Britain by
Hazell Watson & Viney Ltd, Aylesbury, Bucks
Set in VIP Bembo

CONTENTS

EARLY DAYS

This play was first presented at the Cottesloe Theatre, London, on 22 April 1980, under the direction of Lindsay Anderson. The cast was as follows:

KITCHEN	Ralph Richardson
BRISTOL	Norman Jones
MATHILDA	Rosemary Martin
BENSON	Gerald Flood
DOCTOR	Michael Bangerter
GLORIA	Barbara Flynn
STEVEN	Peter Machin

CHARACTERS

KITCHEN
BRISTOL
MATHILDA
BENSON
DOCTOR
GLORIA
STEVEN

SCENE 1

KITCHEN *enters: an elderly man in light summer clothes.*

KITCHEN: Like this. Then this. [*Changes position of hands.*] Then this. [*Relaxes.*] Anything else that you would like? [*Casual. Pause.*] Nothing. [*Waits. Looks round him: glances about him, casual. Then:*] At the sea-side. Travelling in a coach beneath a bridge. I see the bridge, which is really a footwalk, so high above me – it seems I have passed beneath it ever since. I look out of the window of a bus and see the footwalk overhead, so narrow and high on its arched, green-painted metalwork supports . . . that it seems I have passed beneath it ever since. [*Pause: abstracted: gazes out.*] Beyond the bridge is a beach, which lies in a bay which is surrounded by houses: footpaths wind across a hill and lifts go up and down a steep embankment. At some point earlier in the journey I have been left alone on a station platform; or, find that I am alone and those that had been with me are there no longer.

BRISTOL [*entering*]: Do you want your tea, sir? Tea. [*Holds out cup and saucer.*]

KITCHEN: Yes.

BRISTOL: I've brought a table out.

KITCHEN: That's right.

> [BRISTOL *returns with a small wooden table, round.*
> KITCHEN *stands with cup and saucer in hand.*
> BRISTOL *returns with chair, wooden.*]

BRISTOL: Would you like to sit down?

KITCHEN: No.

[BRISTOL *exits: returns with a second wooden chair: sets it at the table.*]

BRISTOL: Would you like me to stay and talk, sir?

KITCHEN: What about?

BRISTOL: Anything you like.

KITCHEN: I was recalling my childhood.

BRISTOL: Anything pleasant?

KITCHEN: Very.

BRISTOL: I – as a child – liked ever-after stories.

KITCHEN: There was never any end to it.

BRISTOL: Ever after means the good things go on for good.

KITCHEN: How can they go on for good?

BRISTOL: Nothing goes on for bad, sir.

KITCHEN: This went on for bad.

BRISTOL: Here you are, then.

KITCHEN: Yes.

   [*Pause.*]

BRISTOL: Anything I can get you?

KITCHEN [*still stands with cup and saucer*]: What's your name?

BRISTOL: Bristol.

KITCHEN: Bristol. [*Turns: hesitates to approach table.*] I was thinking about the sea.

BRISTOL: Yes, sir.

KITCHEN: The first time I saw it I thought the edge of the world had come. I thought the world went on for good. It went on for bad, and came to an end. The sea broke up against the bad, coming down in tiny white crusts. I stood amongst them. The bread ran around and between my toes.

BRISTOL: We all have to come to an end.

KITCHEN: I wonder. [*Pause.*] I walk around the house and I think, 'The people here are mad. They go on as if they know what they're doing.' They don't. No one does.

Yet they go from A to B as if that were precisely what
they intended.

BRISTOL: We all have a destiny to fulfil.

KITCHEN: I wonder. [*Pause.*] Can you smell the blossom?
I've been somewhere else I can never recall – odd sounds,
smells, odd incidents and encounters, occasionally bring
back a fragment, like a headland glimpsed, or a peak of
a mountain: is it a continent, I think, or only an island?

BRISTOL: I travelled far when I was younger.

KITCHEN: I've scarcely travelled at all: to the sea once, but
not much farther. I've endeavoured to live my life in the
place where I started; if I stick to where I start I might
find out (a) where it all went wrong, (b) why I arrived
here in the first place.

BRISTOL: Travelling broadens the mind.

KITCHEN: It narrows it. Jesus never travelled, not more than
a hundred miles; Michelangelo, Rembrandt, Milton: they
are people who made a journey of scarcely any consequence at all and subsequently never travelled farther.
Travel is for people without imagination: dullards, clods;
those who need to animate the landscape otherwise they
see nothing there at all. Are you married? [*Sits: sets cup
on table.*]

BRISTOL: No.

KITCHEN: My daughter is in the house. You can talk to her.
Her husband is at work for most of the day and she has
nothing to do but write her memoirs.

BRISTOL: Yes, sir?

KITCHEN: It's been suggested I should write my memoirs.
I can't remember anything. She is endeavouring to write
them for me. What she can recall of our life together. It's
what I thought you were here for.

BRISTOL: Sir?

KITCHEN: I thought you were someone who knew me.

BRISTOL: No, sir.

KITCHEN: You're not even married.

BRISTOL: No.

KITCHEN: What does your wife do?

BRISTOL: I haven't got a wife.

KITCHEN: Do you remember very much about me?

BRISTOL: I've read about you.

KITCHEN: What have you read?

BRISTOL: Ever since I was a youngster.

KITCHEN: Really. [*Pause: contemplates* BRISTOL.] How long have you known me?

BRISTOL: Only for the past week: while I've been engaged by Mr Benson.

KITCHEN: Who's Mr Benson?

BRISTOL: He's your son-in-law.

KITCHEN: What have you read about him?

BRISTOL: Nothing.

KITCHEN: He was a doctor. Then he went into business. He became a research scientist, discovered a pharmaceutical drug, and was taken onto the board of directors. Subsequently he was appointed chairman of an organization which I heartily despise. I hate wealth, yet I'm unable to do without it. I tried living on my own, in a room, with no one to look after me from dawn till dusk. Finally, my daughter rescued me. When did you know me?

BRISTOL: I don't know you, sir. I was appointed to this post a week ago.

KITCHEN: Are you a spy?

BRISTOL: I was in the army for several years, sir; subsequent to that I was in the catering trade.

KITCHEN: What as?

BRISTOL: I was employed by Mr Benson.

KITCHEN: Who's he?

BRISTOL: He's your son-in-law, Sir Richard.

14

KITCHEN: What's he got to do with it?

BRISTOL: I supervised the company dining-room.

KITCHEN: A cook.

BRISTOL: A manager.

KITCHEN: My daughter is very naïve. She takes other people at the level of her own intentions. I loved her very much when she was young; when she got older I found I didn't know her. What do you do?

BRISTOL: Here, sir?

KITCHEN: As a catering man.

BRISTOL: I arranged the lunches that Mr Benson gave.

KITCHEN: Who to? You can tell me. I'm top-dog. I've ruled the roost here for as long as I remember.

BRISTOL: They were lunches given for executives of the company, and for the personnel of other companies with whom Mr Benson was doing business.

KITCHEN: Why did you give it up?

BRISTOL: Mr Benson offered me the job of being your companion.

KITCHEN: Wasn't the other job good enough?

BRISTOL: I wanted a change.

KITCHEN: Why should you want a change?

BRISTOL: It wasn't going to be a change of a permanent nature.

KITCHEN: What? [*Pause.*] I'm going to die very soon and you can go back to spying on someone else. [*Pause.*] I've found you out.

BRISTOL: Mr Benson wanted someone whom he trusted. I've worked for Mr Benson, sir, for the past twelve years.

KITCHEN: Do they want me to defect?

BRISTOL: No, sir.

KITCHEN: If they pay me enough my memory might start coming back. [*Looks about him.*] I've been thinking of defecting for quite some time.

BRISTOL: Where, sir?

KITCHEN: I exhausted Mathilda through having to keep an eye on me. That's why they had to get in a man. I have a notebook. I leave it on my dressing-room table; Mathilda reads it: she tells her husband. Who is her husband?

BRISTOL: Mr Benson, sir.

KITCHEN: He reads it. What they don't know is that I have a second book which no one reads. Those in there are secret thoughts. Those in there are not for public consumption. What's your name?

BRISTOL: Bristol.

KITCHEN: What a curious name. My name's Kitchen.

BRISTOL: Yes, sir.

KITCHEN: I was remembering my childhood a moment ago. One's childhood is the profoundest period of one's life; after that comes anticlimax. After the age of twenty-one nothing happens again. That is why Mathilda can remember so clearly everything that happened to me between the ages of thirty-five and forty – which to me are a complete blank but which to her are as clear as if they happened this morning. She, when she reaches my age, will be able to recall *my* life more vividly than she can her own. Similarly Gloria – what awful names these women have – will remember her mother more clearly than she does herself. Has my granddaughter been here recently? She's the only person I can talk to.

MATHILDA [*entering*]: I've looked all over the garden for you.

KITCHEN: You shouldn't have such big gardens then I wouldn't get lost.

MATHILDA [*to* BRISTOL]: Has he been all right?

KITCHEN: That man's name is Bristol. He's a German spy.

MATHILDA: The German war has been over, Father, for a very long time.

KITCHEN: He's a Russian spy. He's been encouraging me to defect.

MATHILDA: He's brought you some tea which you haven't drunk. [*Hands tea to* BRISTOL.] I'll look after him a while.

BRISTOL: Right, ma'am. [*Goes.*]

MATHILDA: You shouldn't talk to Bristol as if he were a servant.

KITCHEN: He is a servant.

MATHILDA: He's your companion.

KITCHEN: Is he?

MATHILDA: His wife has divorced him. We invited him here to give him a break.

KITCHEN: He told me he'd been invited here to keep an eye on me. He told me that. He said your husband had instructed it.

MATHILDA: Arthur suggested he might like the job in order to take his mind off things.

KITCHEN: I was going to talk to him about my childhood and you come out here and interrupt. Is Gloria home?

MATHILDA: No.

KITCHEN: Is Arthur?

MATHILDA: No.

KITCHEN: Life is meaningless without your mother.

MATHILDA: Mother's dead, Father. I don't wish to hear any more about it.

KITCHEN: Where she's living I've no idea. [*Pause.*
    MATHILDA *doesn't answer.*]
I met her when I was only sixteen.

MATHILDA: I shan't sit and talk if you refuse to listen.

KITCHEN: You can send that man back. He reports every-thing I say to Moscow. He reports everything you say to Moscow, only what you say isn't that important. I let things drop which the Russians, or indeed the Americans, would pay a very great deal to know. If I charged for it there's no knowing where I'd be. There's so much I have to say, yet there's no one here to listen.

MATHILDA: I listen.

KITCHEN: There's a great deal in that case I'd like to tell you about your mother.

MATHILDA: I don't wish to hear it, Father. I've heard it a dozen times already.

KITCHEN: I seduced her when I was only seventeen.

MATHILDA: I know.

KITCHEN: Did she tell you that?

MATHILDA: You told me that.

KITCHEN: We were married for fifty-five years. If only she'd come back I'd tell her how much I love her. She suspected I didn't: I did. I loved her so much I could never tell her. I could never admit I loved her at all. Why did you die, my dear? [Weeps.] Why did you leave me all alone? [Pause.] How are you getting on with my memoirs, Matt?

MATHILDA: You'll have to get that researcher back.

KITCHEN: How could things that meant so much to me mean nothing to me now?

MATHILDA: You're here to relax, Father. You're here to get better.

KITCHEN: Arthur I've never got on with, Matt. I know you love him and he's everything to you. Perhaps he isn't. Does he have sensations like everyone else? If you don't answer my questions what's the point of my asking them?

MATHILDA: What *is* the point, indeed.

KITCHEN: Now you're getting peaky. I never liked you peaky. Your mother was always peaky. I never cared for it. In a year or two I might be dead.

[MATHILDA *doesn't answer.*]

Is Gloria coming back? I can talk to her like I can talk to
no one else on earth. She despises me. When people
despise me I know where I am.

MATHILDA: We haven't heard from her for weeks.

KITCHEN: I miss her.

[*Pause.*]

MATHILDA: The doctor's coming this morning.

KITCHEN: I don't want to see him.

MATHILDA: You should be grateful he takes so much care
of you. Particularly after the way you treated Madeley.

KITCHEN: Madeley's a sycophant. He wanted to treat me
because I'm a very old man.

MATHILDA: You exhausted his patience.

KITCHEN: A doctor expects to be called at night.

MATHILDA: Not every night.

KITCHEN [*looks away*]: This new man's going to be bored
quite soon.

MATHILDA: He listens very patiently at present, and doesn't
believe a word of it. In addition to which, you haven't his
number.

KITCHEN: I don't believe his name is Bristol; it's a code-
name. Bristol is still a seaport: it has access to America
as well as Russia. The name of the next man will be
Liverpool. Ships will take away my secrets: our secrets;
the secrets you're writing in your memoirs.

MATHILDA: I have a reluctance, Father, to write anything
at all.

KITCHEN: When I'm dead you'll find it easier. Memories
of the dead are easier to come by than those of the
living. Why on earth did you read philosophy? I
thought: my daughter has succeeded by her own
resources in getting to a university which I would have
been proud to get to as a man and the subject she takes

is the most useless one of all. Economics, or history, or even English or one of the sciences. Medicine: you have a great capacity for loving. Medicine, in that case, would have to be out. I talk to your mother here. She seldom listens. I've a feeling she's taken up with someone else. She was always much sought after by other men: 'Why can't *I* have a wife like that?' You could see the complaint on their lips whenever we met: 'I'm condemned to the wife I have while Kitchen here has the best in the land.' She was very loyal; once, she weakened and had a desperate affair: she didn't love the man but I'd driven her into a corner. When it was over she could scarcely stir. She lay crying in the bed, curled up like a mouse. 'Mouse, mouse,' I said. She scarcely heard. I'd have done anything – I *did* do everything – to make her happy. But at the height of my career, just after you were born, I was scarcely home one night in five. She had to cope with you on her own. I had no choice. The roles of men and women were more clearly imprinted on our consciousness than they are at present. Nowadays – we have our Gloria.

MATHILDA: I'll send Bristol out.

KITCHEN: If you got a woman in you could dictate your memoirs. She could type them out, then we could sit under the trees and correct them together.

MATHILDA: Is there anything you want? More tea.

KITCHEN: I'd drink, only everybody hides the bottles; I've tried drugs but they only make me unconscious. Apart from you I've no relief. Who's the man who does the garden?

MATHILDA: Jefferies.

KITCHEN: I gave him a pound last week to buy me a bottle. He never bought me anything. When I accused him of stealing the money he walked away: he was weeding a border at the time and I'm sure he hadn't finished.

MATHILDA: He brought the money to me. Everyone has instructions not to indulge you.

KITCHEN: I can't sleep at night.

MATHILDA: You have your pills.

KITCHEN: You've no idea of the terrors, Matt. If I had a drink they'd go away.

MATHILDA: Drink has been forbidden.

KITCHEN: I'd rather die. I'd rather die right now.

BRISTOL [entering]: Mr Benson's arrived in the house, Mrs Benson.

MATHILDA: That's early.

BRISTOL: Yes, ma'am.

MATHILDA: Did he say why?

BRISTOL: No, Mrs Benson. He's in his study.

MATHILDA: Would you stay with my father, Bristol.

BRISTOL: Yes, ma'am.

MATHILDA: He's being *obstreperous* today.

BRISTOL: Yes, ma'am.

[MATHILDA *goes.*
Pause.]

KITCHEN: Were you really an officer?

BRISTOL: No, sir.

KITCHEN: I thought you said you were an officer.

BRISTOL: No, sir.

KITCHEN: I distinctly heard you say you were an officer in the armed forces.

BRISTOL: I said I was in the army, sir. I was an N.C.O.

KITCHEN: I've made and broken generals. I was in the War Office for seven months; the Board of Trade for over two years. The Ministry of Health for three and a half. What I didn't know about nurses I could write for you on the top of a needle. I'd have got you a commission if I'd known you then. I have no pride. If I had pride I wouldn't be where I am: the most respected political leader of my time who never became prime minister. One speech, lasting twenty-five minutes, and a meeting lasting fifteen seconds, put an end to my career. Are you listening?

BRISTOL: Yes, sir.

KITCHEN: I gather your wife has recently divorced you.

BRISTOL: Yes, sir.

KITCHEN: Have you done something you shouldn't?

BRISTOL: No, sir.

KITCHEN: Why has she divorced you and not the other way around?

BRISTOL: She fell in love with another man.

KITCHEN: How long were you married?

BRISTOL: Fifteen years.

KITCHEN: Almost as long as you've been in service with my son-in-law.

BRISTOL: I married when I came out of the forces, sir.

KITCHEN: I thought you said you weren't an officer.

BRISTOL: There are other people in the army apart from officers, sir.

KITCHEN: Are there? I never met 'em. [*Pause: looks round towards house. Then:*] What did my son-in-law want, coming home at this time? He leads my daughter a dance. He doesn't respect her. How did you feel when your wife went off with another man?

BRISTOL: Not very good, sir.

KITCHEN [*examines him. Then*]: Was the other man married?

BRISTOL: Yes, sir.

KITCHEN: What does he do?

BRISTOL: He's the manager of a building works.

KITCHEN: What sort of building works?

BRISTOL: He builds houses. He was in charge of a house we were having built ourselves.

KITCHEN: Is he living in it?

BRISTOL: I sold it.

KITCHEN: Do you have any children?

BRISTOL: Two.

KITCHEN: How old?

BRISTOL: Twelve and thirteen.

KITCHEN: Are they here?

BRISTOL: They're with my wife.

KITCHEN: If she left you, shouldn't you have them?

BRISTOL: They were happier living with her, sir.

KITCHEN: You keep your feelings under control.

BRISTOL: Yes, sir.

KITCHEN: My son-in-law keeps his feelings under control. It's why he's succeeded in the way he has. [*Looks to house.*] Apart from your marriage do you have anything else to talk about?

BRISTOL: What subject would you care to talk about, sir?

KITCHEN: I had a secretary until a year ago. I can't be left alone with a woman. I had a male secretary, but he got bored. No one writes to me any more. Nothing a politician says has ever been of consequence. The real decisions are made by someone else.

BRISTOL: Who, sir?

[*Pause.*]

KITCHEN: Do you know, I never found out. [*Pause.*] Will you marry again?

BRISTOL: No, sir.

KITCHEN: You sound certain.

BRISTOL: Yes, sir.

KITCHEN: Marriage is the trickiest thing in the world. People disparage it nowadays and treat it lightly; yet marriage is the profoundest experience anyone has.

BRISTOL: You were saying a little while ago, sir, that childhood is the *only* experience we ever have.

23

KITCHEN: You'll find I'm full of contradictions; nevertheless, there's a great deal of sense in them. They say
nowadays it's common for people to marry twice; three
or four times in the circles I move in. I wouldn't describe
those as marriages at all. I'd say they were the cavortings
of disorientated people. Marriage to one person is a
lifetime's experience. It's only through a lifelong commitment to one other person that the depths and the ever
profounder depths that marriage is capable of revealing
are ever experienced. You'll know. Having let this man
go off with your wife you'll find the remainder of your
existence is like a shell: hard, unyielding, with nothing
inside. I believe my talk is distressing you. My advice,
rather than divorce your wife, would be to kill this other
man.

BRISTOL: What if someone doesn't love you?

KITCHEN: She married you. When my wife went off with
another man I injured him so deeply he never looked at
a woman again. He's coming out. That woman in the
village has been complaining.

[BENSON enters: tall, well-built, light suit.]

BRISTOL: Is there anything I can get you, Mr Benson?

BENSON: That's all right, Bristol. I'll just have a word with
Father.

[BRISTOL goes.]

KITCHEN: I've been talking to him about his divorce. It
distresses him. You can see the way he walks. He'll be in
a terrible mood for the rest of the day. If it's to do with
the incident in the village, I've complained before about
the lack of urinals. What are you supposed to do at my
age? I knocked at the house door and the woman refused
to let me in. I told her my name; I got out my wallet. I
showed her the statement of that bank account you won't
allow me to use. All to no purpose: I was compelled to

24

use her wall. *And* she watched me. People have no regard
for age: they see their own destinies far too clearly.

BENSON: Have you telephoned my office?

KITCHEN: I have not.

BENSON: On the recording machine this morning there was
thirty-five minutes of personal abuse.

KITCHEN: That's not very long.

BENSON: The voice is unmistakable.

KITCHEN: I don't know why they employ those machines.
In my days a letter was a work of art. All anyone does
now is scribble.

BENSON: I wasn't told of the tape for over an hour. A thing
like this is never contained. Half the office have heard it
now.

KITCHEN: They may have made a tape of it.

BENSON: They may

KITCHEN: Another tape.

BENSON: I understand precisely what you mean.

KITCHEN: You may be blackmailed.

BENSON: It's hardly likely.

KITCHEN: It's possible. People will stoop to anything for
power or money. I have known men of great importance
in the eyes of the world who would transcribe the
contents of a tape like that as quickly as they would stoop
in the street to a penny. Principles are not involved: life
is amoral; it has no prejudice. Witness my life: spoilt by
one speech and one interview lasting fifteen seconds. I
have had no luck in my life at all; I've been aware of its
indifference from the very beginning.

BENSON: I shall speak to Madeley.

KITCHEN: I don't have Madeley.

BENSON: Why not?

KITCHEN: I don't get on with him.

BENSON: Matt told me he was coming this morning.

KITCHEN: Another.

[*Pause.*]

BENSON: There are worse places you could stay, Father. Without a family atmosphere.

KITCHEN: This place has no atmosphere. It is no family. You with your infidelities have seen to that. One girl is followed by another; one deception by another. Disloyalty is a cancer; it eats out the heart of any marriage.

BENSON: What time is this doctor due?

KITCHEN: I shall acquaint him of the atmosphere existing in this house. I informed Madeley, only he was disinclined to listen. The man is unscrupulous and not to be trusted. I don't like doctors who won't come out at night.

BENSON: You're poisoning your entire existence, Father. Thoughts like these, if they have to be expressed, should be confessed to someone you trust, not confided to a tape machine in someone's office.

KITCHEN: I've had enough of passivity, Arthur. That's Mathilda's philosophy: that's the creed of your long-suffering wife who's borne you a child and stood by you all these years. I have no patience with her. She becomes immobilized. She becomes like Christ.

[MATHILDA *enters.*]

I'm telling your husband, Matt: I'm a man of action.

MATHILDA: We've heard what action, Father. [*Puts down tray with drink.*]

KITCHEN: I don't ask you to listen. Those messages are for your husband alone.

MATHILDA: I've brought you a coffee.

KITCHEN: I hate coffee.

BENSON: The drink is for me.

KITCHEN: Why should he have everything?

MATHILDA [*to* BENSON]: Have you talked to him?

BENSON [*sits, drinking*]: You can see the results.

26

KITCHEN: Why do you give in to this mangling of your loyalty and love? I can't sit here and watch it. How can I see someone I love destroyed?

MATHILDA: I shall have to ask Bristol to take you in.

KITCHEN: He can only take me in if I agree. I intend to resist. I shall shout and scream.

MATHILDA [to BENSON]: Is there anything else you want?

BENSON [looks at watch]: I shall have to go.

KITCHEN: Don't tell me he came home to complain about your father? Disloyalty. Wretch! He's off to betray you with another woman.

MATHILDA: You'll kill yourself, Father, if you go on like this. Arthur's going now because he has to.

KITCHEN: I see.

BENSON [rising]: I want you to bear in mind what I've told you. Mathilda agrees. We can't have our life interfered with in this way. You have your room; you have someone to talk to. You have something to occupy your mind.

KITCHEN: I shall turn up at your factory and give a speech. [To MATHILDA] Speeches have always been my forte; I have the power to sway people which my enemies recognize to this day. Read my history: read my memoirs when they're finally published.

BENSON: If you turn up at the factory I shall have you arrested.

KITCHEN: Will you?

BENSON: I can't put it plainer than that.

KITCHEN: I don't believe you can.

BENSON: I have to go.

KITCHEN: I imagine you must.

BENSON [to MATHILDA]: Shall I see you this evening?

MATHILDA: Yes.

BENSON: I shan't be late. [Kisses her cheek.]

KITCHEN: Torture. New torture! If you saw how your wife waits for you you'd never leave this house again.

BENSON: Goodbye, Father.

[KITCHEN *doesn't reply:*

BENSON *goes.*]

KITCHEN: Why do you let him abuse you?

MATHILDA: He doesn't abuse me.

KITCHEN: You're a woman of sensibility. Of taste. I have never seen a more sensitive child.

MATHILDA: You have a false image of him, Father. My life isn't bound up with Arthur's the way my mother's was with you.

KITCHEN: Promiscuity with him is like a disease: it hangs around him like the air he breathes. Scent, perfume, lotion. Cream. The man is like a fetish. What does he do with all these women?

MATHILDA: He came home especially to see you today.

KITCHEN: You believe he loves me like I love you.

MATHILDA: He does.

KITCHEN: You believe none of these things I say about him.

MATHILDA: It's not your concern.

KITCHEN: You've given him everything, Matt! How can you attract another man? Get rid of him. Men like that are ten a penny. They destroy everything around them, Matt! Believe me. I've seen it!

MATHILDA: I married him twenty-five years ago. I'm too old to start my life again.

KITCHEN: No one's too old. Look at me. I start again. I intend to defect. In Russia there's a home already furnished: it stands in the trees at the edge of a wood. In the evening the sound of singing comes from a nearby village. You can come and join me. At long last, Matt, I shall find some peace.

[*Looks round:*

MATHILDA *has left.*]

Now I have the key to life no one wants to use it. Damned idiot! She'll sit and suffer like her mother.

BRISTOL [*entering*]: Are you all right, sir?

[*No answer.*]

Are you all right?

KITCHEN: I was discussing women's freedom.

BRISTOL: Sir?

KITCHEN: I was discovering my past.

BRISTOL: Anything of interest?

KITCHEN: Very.

BRISTOL: Care to tell me about it?

KITCHEN: You must buy the book. I don't give these things away for nothing.

BRISTOL: You were recalling earlier, sir, an incident at the sea-side.

KITCHEN: Was I?

BRISTOL: The very first time.

KITCHEN: The very first time I was lost on a station. There was a very large crowd. When I turned round my parents had gone. I thought at the time they were gone for good. I cried. All those strange faces were gazing down. [*Pause.*] A few moments later my parents came back. We mounted a bus. It passed beneath a bridge – so high, the people on it looked like flies. So tall, I thought the bridge would fall. Beyond the bridge I saw the sea . . . I was wondering why I was thinking of those early times. It's as if my parents never came back – as if none of our parents ever come back and throughout our lives we stand, looking up at a multitude of faces, not one of which we shall ever know.

[*Fade.*]

SCENE 2

KITCHEN *lies in a chair. The* DOCTOR, *a young, active man,*
35, is taking his pulse: releases wrist.

DOCTOR: That feels fine.

KITCHEN: I'm not fine. I'm ill.

DOCTOR: You sound a bit of a rascal to me.

KITCHEN: It doesn't stop me from being ill.

DOCTOR: That's true.

   [DOCTOR *packs his bag: blood pressure equipment, thermo-*
   meter, etc.]

KITCHEN: You're young.

DOCTOR: Not very.

KITCHEN: To me you're young. You're a boy.

DOCTOR: Not quite.

KITCHEN: How old are you?

DOCTOR: Thirty-five.

KITCHEN: Do you have a practice?

DOCTOR: I have.

KITCHEN: Your father must be rich.

DOCTOR: Not really.

KITCHEN: I don't believe in riches.

DOCTOR: Neither do I.

   [*Pause.*]

KITCHEN: Are you employed by the Government?

DOCTOR: No.

KITCHEN: You've been talking to my daughter.

DOCTOR: I've spoken to Mrs Benson. Yes.

KITCHEN: Has she told you all about me?

DOCTOR: She has.

KITCHEN: Do you live locally?

DOCTOR: I do.

KITCHEN: I never saw you before.

DOCTOR: I never saw you until I came here.

KITCHEN: You've heard about me.

DOCTOR: I have.

KITCHEN: What?

DOCTOR: Everything.

KITCHEN: Really?

DOCTOR: You're the most famous man for miles around.

KITCHEN: Isn't there an author living hereabouts?

DOCTOR: Not famous.

KITCHEN: I thought he was.

DOCTOR: Not really.

KITCHEN [*watches him. Then*]: *I'm* interested in culture.

DOCTOR: Are you?

KITCHEN: I collected pictures. The house is full of 'em. I always picked those that wouldn't last. On the other hand – this author: is he, in your opinion, one of the best?

DOCTOR: I don't believe in choosing the best.

KITCHEN: You've come to the wrong house in that case. This is a house where only the best is good enough. My son-in-law is the best; my daughter *was* the best; my grandchild is about to be the best; I myself was almost the best, only a twenty-five-minute speech and a fifteen-second interview put an end to my career.

DOCTOR: I shall have to be going.

KITCHEN: Stay and have some coffee.

DOCTOR: I've had some.

KITCHEN [*watches him*]: You must have spoken to my daughter for quite some time.

DOCTOR: Fifteen minutes.

KITCHEN: Briefing you.

DOCTOR: That's right.

KITCHEN: The man I had before I didn't like.

DOCTOR: So I heard.

KITCHEN: A sycophant.

DOCTOR: Really.

KITCHEN: He crawled on his knees. You're a runner. I've seen your type before. Life is before you. Don't you believe it. The integral part of anyone's life is always behind them. You'll have been told of my visits to the village.

DOCTOR: I have.

KITCHEN: I'm a sport. I don't like keeping quiet about anything.

DOCTOR: So I gather.

KITCHEN: It's by opening my mouth too much that I lost the opportunity to become the leader of my party. I would have had a coterie of doctors: not one to take my pulse, but six. What do you think to that?

DOCTOR: There's only one pulse.

KITCHEN: Six opinions!

DOCTOR: What if five said 'Dead', and only one said, 'Living'?

KITCHEN: I'd have him sacked. 'Never disagree with medical opinion': it's invariably mistaken. You're not a prevaricator are you?

DOCTOR: I don't think so.

KITCHEN: You're an opportunist! I like that. It's men of integrity I can never stand. You never know what they're really up to.

DOCTOR: I'll look in tomorrow.

KITCHEN: I'm not ill.

DOCTOR: I thought you were.

KITCHEN: Not that ill.

DOCTOR: I'd like to talk to you.

KITCHEN: What about?

DOCTOR: The telephone calls. You can tell me why you make them.

KITCHEN: Why inform me beforehand?

DOCTOR: You can think up an answer.

KITCHEN: Come early!

DOCTOR: I shall.

KITCHEN: Do you have to go?

DOCTOR: I'll see you tomorrow.

[*Goes.*

KITCHEN *watches him, off.*

Pause.]

KITCHEN: I don't like these people who watch from corners.

GLORIA [*enters from opposite side: a young woman of 24*]: I'm not these people. I'm your granddaughter. [*Kisses his forehead.*] Who's that man?

KITCHEN: He's a government agent.

GLORIA: He looks like a doctor.

KITCHEN: He's here to keep an eye on me.

GLORIA: You need more eyes kept on you than anyone I know, Grandpa.

KITCHEN: Are you here to borrow money?

GLORIA: I've come to see you.

KITCHEN: What about?

GLORIA: I'm getting married.

KITCHEN: Have I to be consulted?

GLORIA: Mummy asked me to come and tell you.

KITCHEN: Good.

GLORIA: Is that all you have to say?

KITCHEN: What have I to do? Get up and dance?

GLORIA: You might.

KITCHEN: Here comes Gloriá,
　　　　　　Riding into town!
　　　　　　What shall I give her:
　　　　　　A kiss or a crown!

GLORIA [*laughs*]: I remember!

KITCHEN: When you were young I would take you walking in your pram.

GLORIA: Where did you!

KITCHEN: Round the West End! How people stared! They must have thought I'd stolen you.

GLORIA: I bet!

KITCHEN: Or had a very young mistress!

GLORIA: Most likely.

KITCHEN: My face was famous at the time! It wasn't every man who could push a pram around the West End of London and the very same morning get up in the House of Commons and make a speech on the importance of preserving the art of boxing and other, allied, manly pursuits.

GLORIA [*laughs*]: You're mad!

KITCHEN: When we stayed in the country I would take you across the fields, bumping and bouncing. I would set you beneath a hedge and sit on a tree stump and look at you and say: 'What on earth will become of her?' I devoted more time to you than I did to my daughter. And now, after all these years, she doesn't like me.

GLORIA: I like you a lot.

KITCHEN: How much?

GLORIA: A lot.

KITCHEN: You'd shoot me tomorrow if you got the chance.

GLORIA: I wouldn't.

KITCHEN: The day after.

GLORIA: Never.

KITCHEN: In my father's time they believed in God.

GLORIA: So what!

KITCHEN: Now all you believe in are ideals. As if anything has ever been changed by grasping at one faith instead of another.

GLORIA: 'Don't like my music –
   Don't like my song:
   Don't run away –
   You may have it wrong!'
I remember you when *I* was young – all your little songs
and ditties. Remember your last Party Conference, do
you? [*Sings: 'Men of Harlech'.*]
'Here am I!
Alone and thwarted . . .
Full of hope,
And not down-hearted!'
 [*They laugh.*]
You had a moustache. Quite fancied yourself. Telling
Grandma how the world was made by special people.

KITCHEN: It was.

GLORIA: People like you!

KITCHEN: People like her.

GLORIA: Don't talk to me about Grandma. I know more
about her than you imagine.

KITCHEN: There's that other man back there.

GLORIA: Where?

KITCHEN: In the house. He's an agent in the pay of your
father.

GLORIA: Liar!

KITCHEN: He's promised me a passage to Russia.

GLORIA: Never.

KITCHEN: May I die this instant if what I say is not the
truth! [*Pause.*] I have a cottage waiting for me at the edge
of a wood. In winter the snow lies very deep: the howling
of wolves comes to me as I'm tucked up warm at night.

GLORIA: Bristol is Father's catering manager.

KITCHEN: Is he? [*Looks round.*] I hoped at one time you'd be
like me.

GLORIA: I am like you.

35

KITCHEN: I hardly see it. Who will you marry?

GLORIA: A man.

KITCHEN: Men, I thought, were on the way out.

GLORIA: This is very much a man.

KITCHEN: He sounds like your father. Your mother said the same when she married him. What's he do?

GLORIA: He's a writer.

KITCHEN: Good God. One lunatic in the family is quite enough. Marry a man with a decent profession. Marry a mortician. What's he written?

GLORIA: He's a poet.

KITCHEN [*pause*]: I don't believe it.

GLORIA: I'll give you his book.

KITCHEN: Bring it out here and I'll throw it away.
  [STEVEN *enters.*]

GLORIA: Steven, this is Grandfather.

STEVEN: Hello, sir.

KITCHEN: I don't like people who show respect.

STEVEN: Why, sir?

KITCHEN: I don't like 'em!

GLORIA: He's being mischievous. He doesn't like people who express themselves.

KITCHEN: That sounds like your mother speaking.

STEVEN: We came to tell Gloria's parents that we intend to get married.

KITCHEN: No artist in this world can afford to be married. Marriage is a commitment to life. Art is a commitment to self-aggrandizement. She'll die. There'll be nothing left of her at the end of a month.

STEVEN: I don't believe it, sir.

KITCHEN: You have a job.

STEVEN: Not at present.

KITCHEN: Is she going to keep you?

STEVEN: I intend to teach.

KITCHEN: What's this book she says you've written?

STEVEN: We've brought you a copy. I left it in the house.

KITCHEN [*to* GLORIA]: We had two dogs. I was the only person in the house who didn't want them. Your mother wanted them. My wife, your grandmother, wanted them. It fell to my lot to train them: the women, being sentimentalists, were afraid to touch a hair of their heads. In six months I had them trained to everyone's satisfaction. What with? Force. If I'd succumbed to their intrinsic character our entire life in the house would have become intolerable. I received no thanks; I received abuse. Yet the dogs were trained. Beating and hardship will rid this young man of his poetical aspirations.

STEVEN: It's a desolate world, Sir Richard. No art. No singing. No form of expression.

KITCHEN: I did not construct this world. I was thrust into it, without warning, just like you. Having arrived, I didn't start painting pictures. I took a good look at what I saw. I didn't like it. I made a fuss. I got up and shouted. I became a liability. The world has very few. I became, in short, a pain in the arse. In the arse of the world I deployed my talents.

GLORIA: Take no notice. He's always making speeches. He likes to hear the sound of his own voice. He destroyed his wife.

KITCHEN: I did not.

GLORIA: You destroyed her, Grandpa. Perhaps she asked to be destroyed. Perhaps, on the other hand, she really loved you. However, Grandpa, we're not impressed. We do not approve of your party or its doctrine. The name of your party, old man, is Death.

KITCHEN: Life! Life is what I've lived.

GLORIA: Your achievements, Grandpa, are a pile of dust. The one person who loved you you callously destroyed, by doing those very things you accuse my father of, with your obscene calls and grotesque abuse and your promenading of your genitals in the village street. You used her, Grandpa, but you won't use us.

KITCHEN: You'd better call that doctor back! I won't stand for abuse like that in my house.

GLORIA: It's not your house. It's my house. It's my mother's house. It's my father's house: it's where you live on sufferance!

KITCHEN: You can see what you're letting yourself in for. When I'm dead it'll be you she turns on. That's what you'll have for inspiration! Has he gone? You'd better call that doctor back.

STEVEN: Shall I call him back?

GLORIA: If you shout that catering man is bound to come.

KITCHEN: He's been summoned here to kill me.

GLORIA: Why is he taking all this time?

KITCHEN: He has to make it look like an accident. I'm not complaining. I give him every chance. Don't get married. Kill him instead!

   [*They've gone.*]

I could die out here and no one would know.

BRISTOL [*entering*]: Is there anything you want, sir?

KITCHEN: Have you been listening?

BRISTOL: No, sir.

KITCHEN: All I get are accusations from people who never knew me.

BRISTOL: Yes, sir.

KITCHEN: You can report that back to Moscow.

BRISTOL: Sir.

KITCHEN: They can have that bit for nothing.

BRISTOL: Would you like me to stay and talk, sir?

KITCHEN: I've done with talking. All I wish to see is action.

BRISTOL: Anything I can get you?

KITCHEN: No thanks.

BRISTOL: Will that be all, sir?

    [*No answer.*]

    Sir?

    [*No answer.*

    BRISTOL *goes.*]

KITCHEN: 'Sirs' proliferate here like poison. I won't have it. I don't like it. What are they up to? What have I done? [*Moving off: sees someone coming: comes back.*]

MATHILDA [*entering*]: Where are you off to?

KITCHEN: Those children, Matt, have been insulting me.

MATHILDA: No doubt you deserved it, Father.

KITCHEN: What makes you so vengeful? It won't do either of us any good.

MATHILDA: What makes you so vindictive? It brings out the worst in all of us.

KITCHEN: Has the doctor gone?

MATHILDA: He went some time ago.

KITCHEN: He asked me your name.

MATHILDA: I want you to sit there, Father.

KITCHEN: He suggested you meet him in the village.

MATHILDA: You're incorrigible, Father. I don't know why you do it.

KITCHEN: If these things happen why should I conceal it?

MATHILDA: You'll find soon there'll be no one who will even speak to you.

KITCHEN: What have you to lose?

    [MATHILDA *going.*]

You'll never get the chance again. Give him what he wants. It's like living on an alien planet. I speak the

39

language but no one listens. I make the signs but nobody sees. Is he still watching? [*Looks off to house: turns: straightens tie.*]

Best foot forward:
In with a chance –
Bring out the fiddle
And on with the dance!
[*Dark.*]

SCENE 3

Upstage, sitting around the wooden garden table, are MATHILDA, BENSON *and* GLORIA. STEVEN, *standing by a chair, is reading from a slim book. His jacket is folded over the back of the chair.*

STEVEN: Last night his hair was cut –
　　　and this morning, passing the shop,
　　　he saw the bins being carried out:
　　　across the top

　　　of one was strewn a wad
　　　of hair, the debris of a hundred skulls,
　　　like some eclectic genius gone mad:
　　　grey, brown, black, curls,

　　　strands – a demonic head
　　　carried high across the street
　　　and flung into a cart, crushed,
　　　and driven off . . .
　　　　　　Where do one's debris start?

[*Pause.*]

MATHILDA: I liked that the best!

GLORIA: I preferred the other.

MATHILDA: Don't you like him reading aloud?

GLORIA: Not much.

STEVEN: Prefers me to keep it to myself.

GLORIA: Not really.

MATHILDA: What then?

GLORIA: Don't like him spouting. [*Looks in direction of house.*]

STEVEN: That's the dictatorial side she gets from her grandfather, Mrs Benson.

GLORIA: Is it?

STEVEN: Isn't it just!

[*They laugh.*]

BENSON: What's the title, Steven?

STEVEN: 'Samson'.

BENSON: 'Samson'. [*Runs hand over his hair.*] I could do with a haircut.

[*They laugh.*]

MATHILDA: When I first met your father, he wasn't averse to writing poetry.

BENSON: I copied them out of books, Steve.

MATHILDA: You never told me.

BENSON: You never asked.

MATHILDA: What else did you keep secret?

BENSON: Not much!

[*They laugh.*]

MATHILDA: When I first went to university most of the male students had just come back from the war. Your grandfather didn't like any of them. Your father included.

STEVEN: What regiment were you in, sir?

BENSON: The Medical Corps. I was half-way through school when the war began. I went to university when the war was over. Mrs Benson was studying philosophy then.

MATHILDA: He wrote one of my papers.

BENSON: Not a very long one.

MATHILDA: It gave me a reputation I never lived up to!

[*They laugh.*]

GLORIA: I never knew you were a theorist, Father.

BENSON: I thought at the time it would appeal to your mother.

[*They laugh.*

BRISTOL *enters.*]

MATHILDA: What is it, Bristol?

BRISTOL: Sir Richard's gone, Mrs Benson.

42

MATHILDA: Gone?

BENSON: Gone where?

BRISTOL: I've no idea, sir.

GLORIA: Must be the village.

BRISTOL [to BENSON]: Yes, sir.

STEVEN [picking up coat]: I'll go and look for him, Mrs Benson.

MATHILDA: We'd better all go. I'll call the doctor.

STEVEN: What is it that he's after, sir?

BENSON: He's after power. When he hasn't got it he grasps at everything around him.

MATHILDA: He grasps at us. At times I feel he'll never let go.

BENSON: Oh, he'll let go. He'll have to. He'll not be here for ever.

MATHILDA: He's had an argument with Steve already.

BENSON: We'll shove him in a strait-jacket if we catch him this time.

GLORIA: He's lived in one all his life: he's only now got out of it.

BENSON: I don't know what you mean by that, young lady, and if I did I doubt if I'd agree with it. You go that way, Steve.

STEVEN: Yes, sir.

BENSON: When you find him, Steven.

STEVEN: Yes, sir.

BENSON: Don't let him know he's being followed.

[Light goes down upstage as they leave: comes up downstage as KITCHEN enters.]

KITCHEN: Do I go left?
Do I go right?

Do I go forward?
Or do I go back?

Is this the village I've arrived at, or is it a place I knew as a child?

STEVEN [*entering*]: Have you walked down on your own, sir?

KITCHEN: What?

STEVEN: The village, sir.

KITCHEN: I have an appointment.

STEVEN: Yes, sir.

KITCHEN: I met a young woman the other day. She made all the appropriate signs. She can't be a day over thirty-five.

STEVEN: I'm sorry we quarrelled, sir. Gloria has a dislike of being crossed. Particularly by you.

KITCHEN: I didn't think young men like you believed in marriage.

STEVEN: Yes, sir.

KITCHEN: I thought it went out with the younger generation.

STEVEN: We believe in everything you do, sir.

KITCHEN: Amazing! You're not a psychiatrist, are you?

STEVEN: No, sir.

KITCHEN: Tell me a poem.

STEVEN: What would you like?

KITCHEN: One of your own.

STEVEN: I can't memorize my own, sir.

KITCHEN: Like to hear one?

STEVEN: If you like, sir.

KITCHEN: Here's my Johnny;
       Here's my Jane:
       Two old friends
       Well met again!

[STEVEN *laughs*.]

Good as yours?

STEVEN: Better!

44

KITCHEN: Sin is disfavoured,
    Virtue is blessed –
    Bring in the ladies:
    Let's pick out the best!
 [STEVEN *laughs*.]
STEVEN: Wives can be wise,
    And mistresses pretty:
    One in the country,
    Two in the city!
 [*They laugh.*]
KITCHEN: Oxford, were you?
STEVEN: Yes, sir.
KITCHEN: Public school?
STEVEN: Sir.
KITCHEN: Do much for you?
STEVEN: I ran away, sir.
KITCHEN: What for?
STEVEN: It was an inequitable system, sir.
KITCHEN: I never went to school from the age of twelve. You had it, and objected; I objected, and never had it.
STEVEN: Paths cross, sir.
KITCHEN: In a way. You believe everything that Gloria believes in, do you?
STEVEN: Not everything, sir.
KITCHEN: Give her a gun and not one of us'll be here tomorrow morning.
STEVEN: Gloria believes the world can be made a better place, sir.
KITCHEN: Does she?
STEVEN: It's a belief I share with her, sir.
KITCHEN: All I share with her are blood and bone.
STEVEN: Don't you believe people's lives can be changed to the good, sir?

45

KITCHEN: All the changes that I've seen have been to the bad.

STEVEN: That's a pessimistic view, which very few people could live with, sir.

KITCHEN: I live with it! I've lived with it for as long as I remember. The only relationship that counts is the one we hold with one another. In trust. For ever! [*Moves on.*]

STEVEN: I'll walk with you through the village, sir.

KITCHEN: They've sent you out to follow me.

STEVEN: No, sir.

KITCHEN: I can see you all sitting there. Devising plans. I'm not a fool. Even if I look like one. Damn!

MATHILDA [*entering*]: Are you out with Steven, Father?

KITCHEN: What did I tell you? I can't go out without being followed.

BENSON [*entering*]: Are you on your way out, Father, or on your way in?

KITCHEN: I was walking to the village. I have an appointment. Am I to be allowed nowhere without a guard?

MATHILDA: No one has any designs on you. We'll walk back home with Steve. [*Links her arm with* STEVEN'S.]

STEVEN: Goodbye, sir.

[KITCHEN *watches them go.*]

KITCHEN: What are they up to? [*Watches them further: looks about him.*] Where have they gone?

[DOCTOR *enters from opposite side.*]

DOCTOR: What are *you* up to?

KITCHEN: Who are you?

DOCTOR: I'm your doctor. I'm off to the pub. Do you fancy a drink?

KITCHEN: I was coming down to fetch you.

DOCTOR: What for?

KITCHEN: My daughter has formed a profound attachment for you.

DOCTOR: Has she?

KITCHEN: She is a doctor of philosophy and has set aside her talents for the sake of her family.

DOCTOR: Really?

KITCHEN: She would welcome a lover.

DOCTOR: I'm married.

KITCHEN: What has that got to do with it?

DOCTOR: I have a family of my own.

KITCHEN: No one will know. While the domestic staff are under the impression you are attending to me you can be wrapped in my daughter's embrace in the adjoining room.

DOCTOR: Come for a drink.

KITCHEN: I'm not allowed to drink.

DOCTOR: I'll buy you a fruit juice.

KITCHEN: I hate fruit. Seize this chance! Come early. I'll persuade her husband to leave by seven o'clock.

DOCTOR: Do you feel all right?

KITCHEN: I've never felt better!

DOCTOR: Walk with me to the pub.

KITCHEN: No thank you.

DOCTOR: Let me help you.

KITCHEN: It's not help I need, you fool! It's action!

BRISTOL [entering]: There you are, sir.

KITCHEN: You see! He's been sent out to find me!

BRISTOL: Mrs Benson asked me to come down, sir. She thought you might need an arm to lean on on the way back up.

KITCHEN: I need no arm.

DOCTOR: If you won't have a drink, and you won't have a talk, is there anything I can do for you?

KITCHEN: I've given you my suggestion. What have you to lose?

DOCTOR [*to* BRISTOL]: I should take him back to the house.

    [*To* KITCHEN] See you.

    [*Goes.*]

KITCHEN: The man's a fool. He's not to be trusted. Anyone who pursues decency in public must lead a disreputable private life. How much do you want?

BRISTOL: How much, sir?

KITCHEN: It's only a short walk to my appointment. I'll be in the garden inside five minutes. Look at that window: a man beating his wife. Or is it a carpet? He's waving his arm – he's waving to me! There, I knew! [*Waves back.*] Fame has not eluded me yet. It was his wife I approached the other day. I like *her*!

BRISTOL: That's your granddaughter, sir.

KITCHEN: Is it?

    [GLORIA *enters.*]

GLORIA: You've been very naughty, Grandpa.

KITCHEN: I didn't notice. [*Looks behind him.*]

GLORIA: You created a commotion when you disappeared. [*Links her arm to his.*] You're not to be allowed on your own. You don't behave.

KITCHEN: I don't think anyone loves me. I don't think anyone cares. Your grandmother loved me. Ellen loved me. She sacrificed her life. I can scarcely stand.

GLORIA: It's all right, Grandpa. I'll send Bristol up to the house for the car.

BRISTOL: Right.

    [BRISTOL *goes.*]

KITCHEN: I was dreaming of a journey I took as a child. A bridge so high you could scarcely see it – and the sea . . . I know at some point it will come to an end. What will the sum add up to? Will it be sufficient to get me by? Will

48

it allow me to climb to the top? Will it give me back the love I lost?

[*Light fades.*]

SCENE 4

KITCHEN *is seated in his garden chair: the round table and another chair are at hand. Eyes closed.*

STEVEN *enters.*

GLORIA [*entering*]: What do you think to him?

STEVEN: He's ill.

GLORIA: He's very ill. He doesn't know it.

STEVEN: What has the doctor said?

GLORIA: He's only another few months to live.

STEVEN: Where does he come from? Where did he start?

GLORIA: His father was a grocer. On another occasion, Grandpa told us, he mended watches. After that he was unemployed. Grandpa went out to work at twelve. He ran errands: he bought a shop. He went into politics when he was twenty-five. He joined the wrong party. At that time it believed in breeding. If he'd had a little he might have got on farther. He was the longest serving Minister of Health. Then he made a speech which was critical of his colleagues. He became a dark horse: people mentioned him when they thought of an alternative leader: he was on the ballot paper for the party-leadership two years after the war and came out third; when the time came to make his challenge he'd lost support. The pages of history closed on Grandpa: he was given a knighthood and went into his act of being a cantankerous figurehead whom younger men looked up to and older men despised. Now he is the eldest: those who knew him are dead; there's only you and I to criticize.

[*They leave.*

KITCHEN *wakes.*]

KITCHEN: Am I dreaming? Or do I imagine that? Beddoes!
Meadows! Bristol!

[BRISTOL *enters.*]

BRISTOL: Yes, sir.

KITCHEN: How are your children?

BRISTOL: They're well, sir.

KITCHEN: They're not dead?

BRISTOL: No, sir.

KITCHEN: Your appointment is for scarcely any time at all.

BRISTOL: Yes, sir.

KITCHEN: This chair will be empty. You will be able to
walk about the lawn in freedom.

BRISTOL: Sir?

KITCHEN: A man came to interview me the other day. He
brought a camera. He asked me about people I should
have known; the great occasions of which I'd been a
witness; the private moments behind closed doors. I
couldn't remember. It was all a blank. I said: 'If you don't
move soon you'll be caught by the tide.' He said: 'We are
thirty-four miles inland. Where is the tide?' 'The tide,' I
said, 'is at your heels.' He never stirred.

[MATHILDA *enters.*]

MATHILDA: I'll keep an eye on him for a while.

BRISTOL: Yes, ma'am. [*Goes.*]

MATHILDA: Shall I move your chair?

KITCHEN: No, thank you.

MATHILDA: Into the shade.

KITCHEN: No thanks.

MATHILDA: The sun's going down.

KITCHEN: It is.

[MATHILDA *moves away: sits.*]

They come and go like ghosts. I scarcely see them.
Smoke rises from a fire at the end of the garden. Lit by
that man who runs away when I offer him money. More

sure of his job than he is of me. Soon I shall have to rise with it. All I'll have left will be a handful of dust; a handful of chemicals with which I began, in a backstreet shop, in an industrial town . . . She's gone into the house. No she hasn't. She's sitting over there.

MATHILDA: Are you calling, Father?

[*No answer.*]

KITCHEN: Have those trees moved? What's happened to the house? That fire, Mathilda, is out of control! No it isn't. The man who runs away when I offer him money is stoking it with leaves. *Keep it burning! Preserve the flames!* Where's that spy! He should be here!

[BRISTOL *enters: glass on tray.*]

BRISTOL: Sir? [*Sets glass on table.*]

KITCHEN: What seaport do we leave from? Is this cottage at the edge of the wood, or is it amongst the trees? When the peasants sing in the evening are they from the village, or are they gypsies? Are gypsies allowed there? Are people free?

BRISTOL: Is there anything I can get you, Mrs Benson?

MATHILDA: No, thank you. [*Shakes her head.*]

KITCHEN: Are you ashamed of working for me?

BRISTOL: No, sir.

KITCHEN: What about the children?

BRISTOL: I doubt if they know who I work for, sir.

KITCHEN: Don't they know my name?

BRISTOL: No, sir.

KITCHEN: Do they know anything about me?

BRISTOL: No, sir.

KITCHEN: Do they know that I exist!

[*Pause.*]

BRISTOL: No, sir.

[KITCHEN *picks up glass.*]

MATHILDA: That'll be all, Bristol.

BRISTOL: Yes, ma'am. [*Goes.*]

KITCHEN: 'Will that be all?' 'Is there anything else?' [*Sets glass down, undrunk.*

Light fades, strengthening around his figure.]

I can't see you if you stand behind. I was telling Matt . . . So tall, I thought the bridge would fall. So high, the people on it looked like flies. [*Pause: looking up.*] All those strange faces gazing down . . . Ellen . . . [*Turns.*] Ellen!

[*The light, which has accumulated around his figure, is suddenly extinguished.*]

SISTERS

This play was first presented at the Royal Exchange Theatre, Manchester, on 12 September 1978, under the direction of Eric Thompson. The cast was as follows:

MRS DONALDSON	Noël Dyson
ADRIENNE	Jennifer Hilary
CAROL	Natasha Pyne
TOM	Paul Kelly
BERYL	Pauline Moran
JOANNA	Anita Carey
TERRY	Paul Copley
CRAWFORD	Malcolm Terris

CHARACTERS

MRS DONALDSON
ADRIENNE
CAROL
TOM
BERYL
JOANNA
TERRY
CRAWFORD

ACT ONE

The living-room of a parlour house: i.e., a council house that has
both a downstairs sitting-room and a living-room, in addition to
the large entrance-hall and a kitchen downstairs, and a bathroom
and three bedrooms upstairs.

The living-room, which would normally accommodate a dining-
table as well as easy chairs, now serves in this particular house as
the sitting-room in a conventional middle-class house.

In fact the room has some justification for being described as
middle-class: its two single windows looking out to the garden and
the road are draped with velvet curtains, with a velvet pelmet
above; the furniture, comprising two easy chairs and a settee, has
some pretensions to comfort as well as taste and all three items are
well endowed with cushions as well as their backs being protected
by lace doilies. The sideboard is of a simple but not unpleasant
design and in addition to a tray of bottles and decanters holds a
modern gramophone. There is a low coffee-table in front of the
tiled fireplace holding several magazines and newspapers, and a
folding table at the back of the room, covered by an embroidered
cloth, holds a vase of flowers. Three realistic paintings hang on
the wall: a portrait of a Chinese lady, a landscape containing
fields and woodland, and a sailing-ship – all reproductions slimly
framed.

The atmosphere of the room is restful: the interior is neat, tidy,
fresh, and everything that can be polished and dusted has been; the
feeling is of an extremely clean receptacle waiting for someone to
come into it.

The door which leads out to the hall and the stairs is opened.
A second door leads out to the kitchen.

MRS DONALDSON enters.

She's a matronly woman in her late fifties, working-class in origin, slightly stout, but with a pleasant temperament, homely, intimate, neatly dressed in a plain dress over which she wears a half-apron: her arms are bare to just above her elbow and in her hand she carries a door-key.

She holds the door.

MRS DONALDSON: Come in. Come in.

After a moment ADRIENNE *enters. She's a woman of thirty, perhaps thirty-two or -three; she wears a dark coat with a fur-trimmed collar, high-heeled shoes, and her hair is evidently well looked-after; her appearance, in its general impression of 'style', is countered slightly by the rather worn expression of her features. She gazes round at the room, pausing at the door: she is, acutely, a person of a nervous disposition and inclined — needing, even — to lay stress on her first impressions. Her surveillance of the room is intense, wincing, sharp. She carries a leather suitcase in addition to a leather handbag.*

MRS DONALDSON: Carol isn't at home at present. But I'm sure if you say she's expecting you she will be. She never lets anything slip like that. [*Pause.*] I'm her mother.

ADRIENNE: Her mother?

MRS DONALDSON: My name's Mrs Donaldson. I live in the house next door. I'll take that. Don't want it cluttering up the room, now do we. [*Takes case from* ADRIENNE's *hand and goes out to hall.*

ADRIENNE *steps into the room further: she's wearing leather gloves which, after a moment, still gazing round, she begins to take off.*

MRS DONALDSON *comes back in.*]

Do you like it?

ADRIENNE: Yes. [*From the room she gazes at* MRS DONALD-

SON *who in turn is gazing back at her with a great deal of pleasant animation.*] I'm Adrienne Stanforth.

MRS DONALDSON: Adrienne. I like that. That's an elegant name.

ADRIENNE: Did you say you were Carol's mother?

MRS DONALDSON: That's right. I'll take your coat. I keep the fire laid even though we have the central heating. I don't normally light it until the evening. A room without a fire isn't anything. I've still got the old range in my house next door: the ones we had years ago when the houses were built. I still bake bread in my oven. [*Having helped* ADRIENNE *off with her coat she takes it to the hall door.*] I won't be a minute: I have a hanger outside. [*Goes. Calls*] Sit down. Make yourself at home.

[*After a moment's pause* ADRIENNE *sits: she feels in her bag after a further moment, quickly, involuntarily, and brings out a lighter and cigarettes: she's lighting the cigarette with the same quick movement as* MRS DONALDSON *re-enters.*]

There. Well. [*Reaches immediately for an ash-tray: sets it down on the coffee table.*] I smoked once myself. I'm on my own, now, since my husband died.

ADRIENNE: I'm sorry.

MRS DONALDSON: Five years ago. I don't think I shall marry again. If he came back tomorrow I'm not sure I would know what to do with him: you get so used to living on your own, whereas with a man around . . .

[*Gazes at her with some pleasure and anticipation.*]

ADRIENNE: I'm Carol's sister.

MRS DONALDSON: Here. Let me give you a kiss, then, love! [*Leans down to her and embraces her:* ADRIENNE *half-heartedly responds.*] You can call me Mother as well. Mrs Donaldson always sounds like the head of some department and my first name, Maureen, I really dread. 'More' is what some people call me, so 'Mother' comes fairly easily after that.

ADRIENNE: Why does she call you 'Mother'?

MRS DONALDSON: I *am* her mother! [*Laughs, leaning down to her: sits beside her: takes her hand.*] Not really, love. But everything else. I think Carol's the most wonderful person I've ever met. If I'd had a daughter, Carol is exactly as I would have had her.

ADRIENNE [*after a moment, gazing at her, withdraws her hand*]: Yes. [*She looks round for the ash-tray: taps the cigarette.*]

MRS DONALDSON: Her sister! She never said. She tells me *everthing* before it happens.

ADRIENNE: I came a day earlier, as a matter of fact. [*Nervously.*]

MRS DONALDSON [*sensing trouble*]: Then that'll be it. Though even then it's very odd.

ADRIENNE: I got a cab from the station. The driver didn't know the name of the road.

MRS DONALDSON: They employ anybody nowadays. They even hire cabs out to drivers – battered old vehicles they are, too – and the driver rents them, then has to take everything he can earn. They drive like mad: the insides are in a terrible condition, because they're not responsible for maintaining them. They have no respect for their customers and drop them in all sorts of unlikely places.

ADRIENNE: This one told me it was Waterton Road. When he'd gone I discovered it was a different road entirely.

MRS DONALDSON: They don't like this estate. It's so large for one thing and there are so many little roads and crescents that half the people they employ don't even know their way. I had to tell one driver one day where Beaumont was itself: an estate with over fifteen thousand people which, when it was built, they said was the largest in the country. And then there's the tips: if you tell the

62

driver 'Beaumont Estate' he knows you're going to tip him scarcely anything at all so apart from the journey there's nothing in it for him. He wants to get back to the station as quickly as he can to pick up some businessman or someone who lives at Dalton where the really big houses are. Carol wants to live out there. One day she will: once she sets her mind to something she never looks back. Though she's far too easy-going for my mind. She'd let this place go if I didn't look after it: she's so careless and so absent-minded. That, of course, and her devotion: she idolizes that man, though she's anxious not to show it. Well. That's enough about me. All that talk. Would you like a cup of tea? Would you like something stronger? [Looks to sideboard: ADRIENNE looks over suddenly too.]

ADRIENNE: I wouldn't mind.

MRS DONALDSON: Whisky. Gin. Vodka. A martini.

ADRIENNE: I think a vodka if you've something to go with it.

MRS DONALDSON: Tonic. I think I'll have a nip myself. It's not often we have a day like this. [Gets two glasses out of sideboard cupboard.] And how far did you have to walk, carrying that?

ADRIENNE: It must have been two roads away. Though all the houses look the same.

MRS DONALDSON: They do. [Pouring drink.] Though after you've lived here as long as I have, each one acquires its individual features. You'd be surprised: to me, though they are the same, they're like a crowd of very different people – not so much strangers as individuals. [A drop of tonic.] I've made it stiff. If you want it stronger or weaker you only have to say.

ADRIENNE: Thanks.

MRS DONALDSON: Adrienne. That's a lovely name. I

wonder why she never mentioned it. She tells me
everything. Or nearly everything. She doesn't often talk
about her mother and I don't think, except once, she's
ever mentioned you. And that was how long ago?
Perhaps two years.

ADRIENNE: Yes.

MRS DONALDSON: You're older, of course.

ADRIENNE: Yes.

MRS DONALDSON: Do you like the curtains?

ADRIENNE: Yes.

MRS DONALDSON: I chose them. The furniture, too. She
likes to have me with her when she shops: 'You come,'
she says, 'you're so common, Mother!' [*Laughs hugely.*
    ADRIENNE *watches her: drinks deeply.*]
Well. She should be back any time now. Tom's at the
boozer. He goes down at opening and comes back at
closing.

ADRIENNE: What does he do?

MRS DONALDSON: Do?

ADRIENNE: What's his job?

MRS DONALDSON: He used to be a sportsman. A professional. He was quite famous in his time.

ADRIENNE: What sort of sport?

MRS DONALDSON: Football. After that he became a
labourer. At Harcrofts. Have you heard of Harcrofts?

ADRIENNE: No.

MRS DONALDSON: It's the large steelworks at the edge of
the town: you can see its furnaces when you come in on
the train.

ADRIENNE: Does he work there now?

MRS DONALDSON: Tom? Oh, no. That was what? Four
years ago now. They've been married how long?

ADRIENNE: Seven.

MRS DONALDSON: Five, love. It must be five.

ADRIENNE: It seems longer.

MRS DONALDSON: That's marriage! [*Laughs pleasantly again.*] Would you like to wash? The loo's in the bathroom at the top of the stairs.

ADRIENNE: I wouldn't mind another drink.

MRS DONALDSON: I'll get it, love. One's my ration. Mid–afternoon isn't my normal time.

ADRIENNE: I'll pop upstairs: I won't be a minute.

MRS DONALDSON: First on the left. [*Watches her go.*

ADRIENNE *takes her handbag.*

MRS DONALDSON *gets drink: sets it down on coffee-table: examines* ADRIENNE's *leather gloves which she's left lying there: a hole in one of the fingers: instinctively puts her own finger through.*

Back door of house opens: looks up: listens for step.

After a moment CAROL *enters from kitchen door: wears coat: a fresh, energetic, extremely feminine woman of twenty-five: well-dressed, bright, vivacious.*]

CAROL: Well, then, Ma? Knocking it back at this time, are you?

MRS DONALDSON: My dear, I've been talking to your visitor.

CAROL: At this time? [*In the process of taking off her coat, looks at her watch.*]

MRS DONALDSON: No one you were expecting. Not today.

CAROL: Who?

MRS DONALDSON: Shan't tell.

CAROL: Out with it.

MRS DONALDSON: Shan't.

CAROL [*stalks* MRS DONALDSON *round settee*]: I'll fetch you one.

MRS DONALDSON: You never will.

CAROL: Shall.

MRS DONALDSON: Shan't.

CAROL: Come here, you old cow.

MRS DONALDSON: I'll 'old cow' you. *And* I'm young enough to do it.

CAROL: You're young enough for lots of things but not for that. [*Drops her coat on a chair.*] A woman. [*Picks up the gloves.*]

MRS DONALDSON: A hole in the finger.

CAROL [*pauses*]: Where is she?

MRS DONALDSON: In the loo.

CAROL [*sniffs glove*]: I don't like the scent.

MRS DONALDSON: I didn't like it but *I* didn't say anything.

CAROL: Who is she?

MRS DONALDSON: Someone evidently you weren't expecting.

CAROL [*Pause: looks up*]: I hope you haven't let in anyone, love.

MRS DONALDSON: Do I ever?

CAROL: I've ordered those chairs. Do you believe it: they take two months to deliver. They have to *make* them before you buy them: that's how exclusive they are.

MRS DONALDSON: Nevertheless they're very good.

CAROL: Nevertheless they are. [*Looks up again.*] Who is it?

MRS DONALDSON: Your sister.

CAROL: Who?

MRS DONALDSON: *Adrienne.*

CAROL [*Pause*]: She wasn't expected until tomorrow. [*Looks up more intently.*]

MRS DONALDSON: *I* was never told. You've scarcely ever *mentioned* a sister.

CAROL: You scarcely ever mention your husband.

MRS DONALDSON: He's dead.

CAROL [*goes to hall door*]: Aid! [*Calls: waits.*] She'll be down in a minute. [*Looks once more at gloves.*]

MRS DONALDSON: The taxi dropped her two roads away.

That must have been in Gold Cross Avenue. She's not very much like you.

CAROL: No.

MRS DONALDSON: But then no one's like you, love, so we can't expect it.

CAROL: No. [*Evidently hears a sound outside: turns apprehensively to the hall door.*

After a moment ADRIENNE *enters: calm, collected: has evidently freshened up: pauses inside the door.*]

ADRIENNE: Hello, Carol.

CAROL: Hello, love. I wasn't expecting you until tomorrow. [*Gazes at her with concern: then, with feeling, crosses to her and embraces her warmly.*] There, then. Let's have a look at you.

ADRIENNE: How are you?

CAROL: I'm lovely. I'm very well.

ADRIENNE: I arrived a day early. There was a confusion of dates and times.

CAROL: That's perfectly all right. That's fine and dandy. Time is what we have an abundance of up here. Let's have a look at you. [*Holds her at arm's length. Then:*] Oh, love. You know, I've missed you. [*Holds her to her.*]

ADRIENNE: I've got a drink somewhere.

MRS DONALDSON: Here it is.

CAROL: This is Mrs Donaldson.

ADRIENNE: We've already met.

CAROL: I call her 'Mother'. I don't know why. She likes to be called it.

ADRIENNE: That's as good a reason as any. [*Drinks.*]

CAROL [*glancing directly at her*]: That's right.

[ADRIENNE *finishes the drink: looks for somewhere to set the glass.*]

MRS DONALDSON [*takes it*]: Would you like another?

ADRIENNE: No. No. [*Hesitates.*] I feel fine.

CAROL: I'd like some tea, More, if you can manage it.

MRS DONALDSON: Right. [*Looks round room: takes up* CAROL's *coat: takes up her own empty glass: looks round for any other: goes out through kitchen door, closing it behind her.*]

CAROL: Sit down, Aid. Are you feeling hungry?

ADRIENNE: I had something on the train.

CAROL: If you'd sent us a telegram I could have met you. I was going to the station tomorrow.

ADRIENNE: Everything happened in such a hurry.

CAROL: Well.

> [*Pause:*
>
> CAROL *gazes at* ADRIENNE:
>
> ADRIENNE *glances at the room.*]

ADRIENNE: It's very cosy.

CAROL: Yes.

ADRIENNE: Not what I'd imagined at all.

CAROL: What had you imagined?

ADRIENNE [*pause: tries to think*]: I'm not sure.

CAROL: Something coarser, as our mother would say.

ADRIENNE: Yes. .

CAROL: I'm not a coarse person.

ADRIENNE: No.

CAROL: Not really.

ADRIENNE: No.

CAROL: Did you get my telegram when our mother died?

ADRIENNE: Yes.

CAROL: Why didn't you come?

ADRIENNE: . . . everything was very confused at the time..

CAROL: I can't see anything less confusing than that.

ADRIENNE: Don't get at me, Carol.

CAROL [*sits beside her on the sofa*]: I'm not being belligerent. I would like to know.

ADRIENNE: I know you were very attached to her.

CAROL: No more than you.

ADRIENNE: I . . . was more attached to Father, really.

CAROL: You never came to his funeral, either.

ADRIENNE: No.

CAROL: You've been rather a naughty girl.

ADRIENNE: I believe I have. [*Laughs, sharply: opens her bag: gets cigarettes and lighter. Starts to take one herself then suddenly offers one to* CAROL.]

CAROL: I don't.

ADRIENNE: Do you mind?

CAROL: Not at all. You can do anything you like here, love!

ADRIENNE: Anything?

CAROL: Anything at all! [*Gestures round: laughs.*]

ADRIENNE: It's so good to see you.

CAROL: Yes?

ADRIENNE: Just to have someone to talk to.

CAROL: There's never any shortage of those.

ADRIENNE: Isn't there?

CAROL: None whatsoever. Talking is what this house is famous for. We keep, Aid, extremely irregular hours.

ADRIENNE: I haven't talked to anyone for a very long time.

CAROL: No one?

ADRIENNE: No.

[*Pause.*]

CAROL: Have things been hard?

ADRIENNE: Not really.

CAROL [*pause*]: When you wrote, two years ago, and said your marriage had broken up – I really, desperately, wanted to talk to you then.

ADRIENNE: Yes.

CAROL: You never answered my letter.

ADRIENNE: No.

CAROL: I wanted to talk to you about Mother. About Dad.

ADRIENNE: Yes.

CAROL: My mother was really upset when you never came to Father's funeral. That was seven years ago now.

ADRIENNE: I would have come. [*Holds her forehead lightly, as if thinking.*] Things were rather difficult then.

CAROL: When mother died a year later I think it was partly due to that.

ADRIENNE [*thinks again, her hand to her forehead*]: I wanted so much to have something to show them.

CAROL: I know, love.

ADRIENNE: I wanted so very much to be a success.

CAROL: We would have helped you.

ADRIENNE: Would you?

CAROL: Why do you under-rate us so much?

ADRIENNE: I don't under-rate you.

CAROL: You were such a dreamer, Aid.

ADRIENNE: I didn't think so.

CAROL: Oh, I don't mean in any passive sense. But those schemes: those wonderful fantasies. Do you remember lying in bed at night: how I'd come into yours when it got very cold and you used to cuddle me and tell me stories?

ADRIENNE: I don't remember that at all.

CAROL [*brightly*]: You must remember. I could never forget a thing like that!

ADRIENNE: I . . . There are so many things I don't remember.

CAROL: Don't want to remember.

ADRIENNE: I was never very happy at home.

CAROL: Weren't you?

ADRIENNE: I do remember. Yes.

CAROL: Do you remember that night: the last Christmas when we hung up a sack for presents: *I* hung up a sack for presents – you were a little bit above it then – and you leaned across to my bed and woke me up? You said, 'Can

70

you hear that, Carol?' And when I raised my head you
said . . . 'Angels.' And from somewhere – it must have
been the end of the road – came the sound of singing: a
choir. It was the most angelic thing I'd ever heard. And
since I was cold you took me into your bed: we lay
together and listened. I believed . . . oh, I believed for so
long I was hearing angels. Christmas night had so much
mystery then . . . that mysterious presence that delivered
presents . . . that preoccupation with the sky and stars,
with goodness and generosity and giving. And do you
remember what you said, lying there? 'The one present
I want I think I might have. Not tonight, another night.'
And when I asked you what it was you said, 'I intend to
go away. I'll become so famous that people will follow
me in the street. Everyone will look: everyone will know
my name. And everywhere I go I shall take you with
me.' I felt so good; I felt so proud: I felt protected. It was
as if it had happened already. You made it so real: the
places we went to: the people who saw us: the cars we
rode in. It was so extraordinary, Aid, that even now,
each Christmas, I think of it. I look out at that sooty
road, with all those identical houses, and think, 'One
day . . . that really will happen.' Out there is a magic I
glimpsed as a child. You *made* me a dreamer: and here
am I accusing you.

ADRIENNE: You were always very practical, Carol. Practicality was your second name.

CAROL: Yes. I'm certainly practical now right enough.

ADRIENNE: What's your husband like?

CAROL: I don't know what you'll think of him.

ADRIENNE: What's that?

CAROL: For one thing, Aid, he's very rough.

ADRIENNE: It's not like you.

CAROL: Isn't it?

71

ADRIENNE: No.

CAROL: How much do you know me really, love?

ADRIENNE: I don't know how well I know you. If I suddenly sound sceptical or belligerent you'd better tell me.

[*Pause*.

CAROL *watches her a moment:* ADRIENNE *stubs out her cigarette, half-finished, and automatically gets out another.*]

CAROL: I've told him all about you, of course.

[ADRIENNE *looks at her.*]

You're our only living relative. He never knew Mother: I met him after she died.

ADRIENNE: I was never invited to the wedding.

CAROL: Would you have come?

ADRIENNE: I think I would.

CAROL: I suppose *I* was feeling belligerent at the time. I thought, 'That *cow*. She's all I've got left. She's gone off to live this wonderful life.' There I was, landed with Father, landed with Mother: both quite ill in their ways and *covered* in debts: Father with his ridiculous schemes for making money and Mother with her endless schemes for spending it.

ADRIENNE: I left home, I suppose, to get away from it. I was eighteen at the time, Carol, and you were what? Twelve? I couldn't stand the delusions: I couldn't stand the mediocrity: I couldn't stand those provincial people with their primness and complacency and their sickening, stifling self-righteousness. I felt if I didn't get out I would never breathe.

CAROL: I missed you so much.

ADRIENNE: You were the one I missed too. I really would have sent for you. I really would.

[*Pause:*

ADRIENNE *is about to speak.*

72

Door opens from the kitchen: MRS DONALDSON *enters with tray.*]

MRS DONALDSON: Well, then, my dear: are you having a chat. I can light the fire if you like.

CAROL [*looks to* ADRIENNE. *Then*]: No thanks, Ma.

MRS DONALDSON: *Mother.* Mother, is what I want. I've brought some biscuits. I'll just go fetch the teapot, love. [*Goes.*
Tray contains two cups and saucers, biscuits and plates: sugar bowl, teaspoons, and milk-jug.]

ADRIENNE: She's a very odd woman.

CAROL: Do you think so?

ADRIENNE: She idolizes you.

CAROL: She's very affectionate.

ADRIENNE: Do you employ her?

CAROL: I give her a little. She does it for the company more than anything else. Like me: she hasn't any living relative: at least, that keeps in touch.
[MRS DONALDSON *comes back in: teapot covered by a tea-cosy.*]

MRS DONALDSON: If there's nothing else, love, then. I'll go on back.

CAROL: You can stay if you like.

MRS DONALDSON: I think two sisters who haven't seen each other all these years deserve a little bit of time together. *He'll* be coming back in any case quite soon.

CAROL: Thanks for the tea, love.

MRS DONALDSON: Right. [*Hesitates, glancing at* CAROL.] All right. [*Nods at* ADRIENNE, *rather sadly, then goes.*]

ADRIENNE: She seems a bit jealous.

CAROL: Do you think so? [*Pouring tea.*]

ADRIENNE: I think so.

CAROL: Do you like it with milk?

ADRIENNE: All right.

[CAROL *hands her a cup.*]

CAROL: Have another drink if you want to.

ADRIENNE: No. No. This is fine.

CAROL: I haven't got your room ready yet. I'll ask More to come in later. How long do you think you're going to give us?

ADRIENNE: I . . . don't know yet.

CAROL: There's all the time in the world up here. I suppose it brings back a lot of memories. [*Gestures out.*] It's not unlike where we lived before. I thought I'd move here after Mother died: it was Tom's house. He'd been married before.

ADRIENNE: I didn't know.

CAROL: It didn't work out. He's three years older than me. He got married when he was only eighteen. The woman herself was twenty-three. He's a bit of a fantasist as well. It doesn't often show, however. [*Laughs.*

    ADRIENNE, *having taken one drink of the tea, has put the cup back on the coffee-table.*]

What have you been doing the last couple of years?

ADRIENNE: Oh. Drifting.

CAROL: I saw your husband has made a name for himself.

ADRIENNE: He did.

CAROL: After you left him.

ADRIENNE: He left me as a matter of fact. [*Quickly.*] It was just as well. I arranged it that way so he wouldn't feel bad. I could see it wouldn't work and that he hadn't the strength to get out himself, or to face the fact that I would have left him, so I made life for him so dreadful he finally plucked up the courage. A year later he took a small part in a film – through someone I knew who arranged it for him – and a few weeks later, by a pure stroke of luck, the star who should have played it fell ill and, because he'd impressed them all so much, they offered it to him.

74

People said I'd held him back: if they'd known him before he met me anyone with discernment would have seen how much I'd brought him on. I taught him everything. However . . . I'm glad he has done well. Even though he wouldn't have it in him to acknowledge it. It's a very hard world, Carol. [*Stubs out her cigarette: hesitates about getting out another.*]

CAROL: Have you been working?

ADRIENNE: Sort of.

CAROL: I'm having some friends coming round in a while. I was going to give you a little room at the back: it's quite cosy and it's away from the noise.

ADRIENNE: I noticed you'd got a bedroom downstairs. In the other room.

CAROL: Yes.

ADRIENNE: It's normally the sitting-room in these parlour houses, isn't it?

CAROL: This is usually the living-room. If we eat, we have it in the kitchen. I've got my washing-machine in a little hut outside! [*Laughs.*] Often our friends stay over: the house, quite frequently, is full of guests.

ADRIENNE: Are you working?

CAROL: I keep picking up odd pieces here and there.

ADRIENNE: Mrs Donaldson said Tom's out of work at present.

CAROL: He works at home.

ADRIENNE: What does he do?

CAROL: He does any number of things . . . that must be him now. [*Slam of front door off, followed by coughing and clearing of throat: a massive sneeze.*

CAROL *has risen:* ADRIENNE *remains seated.*
They gaze at the hall door which opens after a moment and TOM *enters.*
He's a sturdy, open-faced man of twenty-nine, dressed in a

good-quality sports jacket and flannels, with his shirt-neck open.]

TOM: By God, you know: I've picked up summat in that bloody boozer. [*Stops dead when he sees* ADRIENNE: *gazes at her a moment. Then: nods at her.*] Who's this?

CAROL: This . . . after all these years – is my older sister.

TOM: I thought she wasn't coming until tomorrow.

CAROL: She came today.

TOM: How are you?

ADRIENNE: All right.

TOM: You needn't get up. [*She hasn't: he comes to her and shakes her hand perfunctorily.*] Is that tea? [*Looks round for cup.*]

ADRIENNE: You can have mine, if you like. I've scarcely touched it.

TOM: You don't mind me drinking after you, then?

ADRIENNE: That's up to you. It's you, after all, who stand to be poisoned.

TOM: Another joker. I thought thy sister wa' the joker in the family, then. [*Drinks* ADRIENNE's *tea.*] No sugar. [*Almost chokes.*]

ADRIENNE: I don't take sugar.

TOM: Another of her idiosyncrasies is that. [*Puts sugar in remainder: stirs it up.*] Well. I'll leave you to it. [*Drinks.*]

CAROL: Where are you going?

TOM: I don't know. Where do you want me?

CAROL: You can stay and talk. It's not often you have your sister-in-law to see you.

TOM: It's not ever, thank God. [*To* ADRIENNE] No disrespect to you. But one of her is one enough.

ADRIENNE: You needn't stay, Tom, if you don't want to.

TOM: I don't mind staying: I don't mind going. [*To* CAROL] What do you want?

CAROL: Pour me another cupful before you take any more yourself.

[TOM *is about to pour into his own cup: pours into hers. They wait: he finally sits down: drinks his tea after stirring it.*]

We were talking about the past.

TOM: Were you?

CAROL: I was reminding Aid of that time at Christmas when I thought there were angels in the street outside.

TOM: She still thinks there is if she looks long enough.

ADRIENNE: I came up a day early, I'm afraid. If it puts out your plans I don't mind staying at some hotel.

CAROL: You'll do no such thing.

ADRIENNE: I left some other luggage at the station.

CAROL: Tom'll fetch it. [*To* TOM] Have you been to the pub?

TOM [*doesn't answer. Then*]: What was the weather like?

ADRIENNE: Where?

TOM: Where you've come from.

ADRIENNE: It's been all right.

TOM: I hear your husband's turned into summat.

ADRIENNE: My former husband.

TOM: You're divorced, then, are you?

ADRIENNE: Yes.

TOM: Don't talk to me of divorce. I've got a first wife who bleeds me, for one.

CAROL: She doesn't get much out.

TOM: That's quite correct.

CAROL: Blood out of a stone is an impossibility.

TOM: Thy married me quickly, so there must be summat there.

CAROL: There must be. And I'm very fond of it.

TOM: I think I'll go upstairs and read.

77

CAROL: You'll do no such thing. [*To* ADRIENNE] He never reads.

TOM: When's Joanna and Beryl coming, then?

CAROL: Any time.

TOM: Anyone booked in?

CAROL: I believe there are. [*Glances from* TOM *to* ADRIENNE. TOM *glances from* CAROL *to* ADRIENNE *then back again.*]

TOM: If you've got your left-luggage ticket I can nip up to the station now.

ADRIENNE: It's in my bag.

[TOM *reaches over and gets it, handing it to her.*
ADRIENNE *searches it: takes out ticket.*]

TOM: How much is there?

ADRIENNE: A trunk.

TOM: I s'll need a taxi.

[ADRIENNE *explores bag again for money.*]

CAROL: He'll pay for it. Now don't be so silly. [*To* TOM]

TOM [*standing*]: How long are you thinking of staying, then?

ADRIENNE: I don't know.

CAROL: I'm giving Adrienne the room at the back.

TOM: Well it's quiet enough there. [*Pauses on way to the door.*] Are you working at present?

ADRIENNE: No.

TOM: Right. [*Glances at* CAROL.] I'll see you shortly. [*Goes out of hall door, closing it behind.*]

ADRIENNE: There are one or two things shortly coming up. It's why I can't be sure how long I can stay.

CAROL: It doesn't bother me, love. I hope they don't come up: I shall see more of you. As for Tom: he's very brusque but he means very well. He'll come back in a minute before he goes. [*She waits: gazes at the door.* ADRIENNE *gazes at it also.*

After a moment it opens and TOM *comes back in.*]

78

TOM [*leans down to her: kisses her cheek, and then her lips:* ADRIENNE, *watching, glances away*]: See you again, then. [*To* ADRIENNE]

ADRIENNE: Right.

[TOM *nods: goes.*]

CAROL: His first wife nearly killed him.

ADRIENNE: How?

CAROL: He had an eye for other girls. He still has: I know how to keep him in line, however. He's very keen to make a go of it. And one day: well, we won't have to live like this.

ADRIENNE [*looks round suddenly*]: You haven't got a telephone?

CAROL: Can't.

ADRIENNE: Why not?

CAROL: Everyone would use it. There was a woman at the end of the road had one installed: there were people at her door all day. *She* had it put in for her invalid mother who lives the other side of town, and she had it there in case she called her: nett result, with people clamouring to use it, she had to have it taken out. There's nothing so important that a letter or a message brought to the door won't do.

ADRIENNE: No.

CAROL: People know you're here then, do they?

ADRIENNE [*hesitates*]: I left the address. And I can always ring myself.

CAROL: There's a coin-box at the end of Gold Cross Avenue. I know, you think we're primitive.

ADRIENNE: Not at all.

CAROL: Those dreams you always had. It's still waiting, love. That door is waiting to be opened: one day it will. I read the papers every day. Hoping to catch a glimpse of you.

ADRIENNE: Yes.

CAROL: It'll happen. It was you who gave *me* a vision. Not as grand as yours. But one day I'll get out of this. I'll have a detached house at Dalton, two cars, a view of the castle, and live such a life. Well: you'll be able to picture it for me better than I can myself.

ADRIENNE: You'd still live here, then.

CAROL: The big cities aren't for me. I don't like anonymity. It's small and squalid here at times, but the people are pleasant: there's nothing going on that no one doesn't know about. Everything's so open. You'll see, one day: you've got bigger dreams than me: you're like an eagle: you've flown to the top of the mountain and seen what lies the other side. Whereas me: I'm still in the foot-hills. It's the thought of you being up there that keeps me going: I'm very much one for the common run of things: but I like to dream: I like to imagine. There's something here I'll never let go.

[*Front door goes, off.*]

There, you see. They're here already. [*Gets up, tapping* ADRIENNE's *arm consolingly.*] I won't be a minute. [*Goes out to hall, closing door behind her.*

ADRIENNE, *left on her own, glances round, looks at the drink on the sideboard: feels for a cigarette: gets packet out: hesitates: fumbles: puts cigarettes back. Gets up: restless: looks about her: goes to window: looks out: distracted: sees nothing: turns.*

As she does so, door opens: BERYL *comes in: a young woman of twenty-three, slender, tenacious, with a provincial toughness: a rather gaunt face which has been manufactured into a coquettish charm. Her clothes are smart, if austere: a skirt just above her knee, boots: a thick woollen jersey, high-necked.*]

BERYL: Hello, love.

ADRIENNE: Hello.

BERYL [*puts out hand*]: You're Adrienne.

ADRIENNE: Yes. [*Hesitates: then as* BERYL *crosses to her shakes her hand.*]

BERYL: Just arrived.

ADRIENNE: Yes.

BERYL: Jo's upstairs taking off her coat. Tea just made then, is it? [*Evidently at home here: leans down casually to feel the pot. Lifts lid.*] Do you want a cup?

ADRIENNE: No thanks.

BERYL: Maureen here then, is she? Mrs Donaldson.

ADRIENNE: No.

BERYL: Shan't be a jiff. Help yourself to a drink if you like.

ADRIENNE: Yes.

[BERYL *goes out to kitchen with teapot.*

ADRIENNE *waits: attention caught by voice calling evidently from hall through to kitchen:* CAROL: 'Jo: for God's sake!' *then women's laughter.* BERYL: 'In there!' *Laughter.*

A moment later hall door opens.

CAROL *comes in: holds door for someone to follow her.*]

CAROL: You've met Beryl, have you?

ADRIENNE: Yes.

CAROL: Here's Jo. [*Calls out of door.*] Jo! [*To* ADRIENNE] They didn't know I had a sister. They *say* they didn't know I had a sister. [*Calls.*] Jo! [*To* ADRIENNE] Has she made some more tea? [*Calls.*] Jo!

[*Laughter off, this time from kitchen.*]

JOANNA [*off*]: She says you've let her have downstairs!

CAROL [*calls*]: I have not. Come in here: I want you to meet someone very special.

[*Pause:*

CAROL *looks at* ADRIENNE: *smiles: grimaces, indicating the women off.*

After a moment JOANNA *enters: she's a small, cheerful,*

81

roundish figure, amply proportioned, wearing a sweater and a pair of jeans. In her early twenties. She enters directly and crosses immediately to ADRIENNE.]

JOANNA: Hello, love. I'm Joanna. Whatever she's told you don't believe. [*Shakes* ADRIENNE's *hand quickly, but genially.*] My hair-brush is missing *and* my eyelashes have gone from the bathroom.

CAROL: You'll have to speak to More. I'm not here to follow you around.

JOANNA: I could do with some tea. I've had no dinner. I'm absolutely starving. [*To* ADRIENNE] I'm on a diet. [*To* CAROL] What's that awful scent you use?

CAROL: It's . . . something new.

JOANNA: Is that the title or the explanation? [*To* ADRIENNE] She has absolutely no discrimination. If someone wasn't here to check, this house would smell like the inside of a sewer. [*Calls.*] Beryl! For God's sake, hurry up. [*To* ADRIENNE] Are you from around here, love?

ADRIENNE: No.

CAROL [*laughs*]: Joanna is someone to whom you *never* confide any of your secrets.

JOANNA: I feel so light. I feel I could float. I'd go up to the ceiling if I let go this chair. Is Tom in?

CAROL: He's fetching Adrienne's trunk from the station.

JOANNA: You here for long then, love?

ADRIENNE: I thought I'd stay . . .

CAROL [*her arm in* ADRIENNE's]: We haven't seen each other for seven years.

ADRIENNE: Longer.

JOANNA: She tells everyone about you, love.

CAROL: Liar.

JOANNA: Yes, you do. Famous personality. *Actress.* The *houses* she described. The cars: the holidays abroad. I've had holidays abroad but I never enjoyed them: if nothing is familiar I don't know where I am. I'm so tired: and I'm so hungry: I've gone for hours without any food. [*Looks round at drinks.*] I could take one of those but I know I shouldn't. [*Looks at tiny watch on her wrist.*] S'only teatime. Oh! [*Stretches: yawns.*] How long did you say you were staying?

CAROL: Adrienne is having the back room, so you needn't go on about that.

ADRIENNE: Do you live here as well?

JOANNA [*glances at* CAROL. *Then*]: I am what may be described as an intermittent paying guest. [*Door opens from the kitchen:* BERYL *comes in with cups and teapot.*] She's another.

BERYL: Another what?

JOANNA: I was describing to Adrienne who you were.

BERYL: Jo has been to college.

JOANNA: I have not.

BERYL: She went to school until she was eighteen and has lots of wonderful things to say.

JOANNA: Bitch.

BERYL: Cow.

JOANNA: Whore.

BERYL: Would you like another cup?

ADRIENNE: All right.

JOANNA: Any *other* biscuits. [*Examining those on tray.*] Anything *very* nice to eat?

CAROL [*laughing*]: I'll go and see. [*Goes out to kitchen.*]

BERYL [*pouring tea*]: How long are you up for, love?

JOANNA: *I've* asked her that already.

BERYL: What did she say?

JOANNA: Mind your own business.

ADRIENNE: I haven't decided how long I'll stay. There are several things I may be called away for.

BERYL: You have a very unpredictable life.

ADRIENNE: Yes.

BERYL: You never know what's happening from one minute to the next. [*To* JOANNA] Do you want a cup of this?

JOANNA: Of course.

BERYL: I'd like to live like that.

JOANNA: I wouldn't.

BERYL: I like the unpredictable. I like the glamorous and the unexpected. I like the floor to open beneath me. I'm a moon character.

JOANNA: She's Leo the lion.

BERYL: I'm Cancer the crab.

JOANNA: You should say so.

BERYL: On some astrologers' charts I'm Cancer. On others I'm Leo. I can't help it if I'm caught between. She's Aries the ram.

JOANNA: I am!

BERYL: Do you take sugar?

ADRIENNE: No thanks.

[BERYL *hands her the cup.*]

BERYL: I like your dress.

ADRIENNE: Thank you.

BERYL: I saw your coat in the hall. It's very nice.

ADRIENNE: Yes.

BERYL: What's it like to be married to a wonderful husband?

ADRIENNE: I'm not married.

BERYL: I thought you were.

JOANNA: Adrienne's divorced.

BERYL: Didn't Carol say she was married?

JOANNA: She said she was. But not any longer. [*To* ADRIENNE] That's what she told us the last we heard.

[CAROL *entering with sliced pieces of cake.*]

CAROL: I had to see More. She collects all our food next door.

BERYL [*to* ADRIENNE]: She does that so we'll have to visit her.

JOANNA: She listens through the wall.

CAROL: She does not.

JOANNA: She puts her head into the fireplace. [*To* ADRIENNE] In these council houses the flues are adjoining: you can hear every word that's said next door.

BERYL: Liar.

JOANNA [*calls to fire*]: Are you listening, Mother! [*She and* BERYL *laugh.*]

CAROL [*smiles at* ADRIENNE]: You can go up, if you like, and have a lie-down. I can easily change the room round later.

ADRIENNE: I wouldn't mind.

BERYL: Do you want your tea?

ADRIENNE: . . . I'll come down and get some later.

CAROL: Come on, love. Up to bed-for-cheers. [*To others*] I won't be a minute. [*Her arm round* ADRIENNE: *they go.*
    Pause.]

JOANNA: Well.

BERYL: The famous paragon.

JOANNA: What's a paragon?

BERYL [*stretches: yawns. Then*]: What time's yours?

JOANNA: Four-thirty.

BERYL: Six o'clock. I was hoping before he came I'd get some kip. Last night was an absolute dead loss.

JOANNA: Chocolate and ginger. [*Cake.*]

BERYL: More gets more, I think, each day.

JOANNA: I'll have a bath before I begin.

BERYL: What's she come up for?

JOANNA [*nibbling*]: Kippers are fattening and I ate one raw. *Practically* raw, this morning. Everything you like is always fattening. [*Looks up, seeing* BERYL *gazing up.*]

BERYL: If you ask me that girl has brought us trouble.
[*Fade.*]

ACT TWO

Evening: the same: room tidy as before: the tray and tea things have been cleared away; the curtains are drawn and the lights are on.

Sitting there, rather tense, is a young man, TERRY, *twenty-three; he wears a corduroy coat and a woollen shirt without a tie, and is looking at one of the magazines: he looks ::p quickly when he hears a sound.*

After a moment the hall door opens.

ADRIENNE *enters: she has evidently recently woken and is in her stocking feet.*

ADRIENNE: Oh.
TERRY: Excuse me. [*Stands up quickly.*]
ADRIENNE [*looks round*]: I was looking for my sister.
TERRY: Who?
ADRIENNE: Carol.
TERRY: She's out.
    [ADRIENNE *blinks in the light.*]
    She went to get some Scotch.
ADRIENNE: Oh. [*Stands there a moment: the mention of drink, clearly, hasn't eluded her.*]
TERRY: My name is Terry. [*Steps forward and offers his hand.*]
ADRIENNE: I'm Adrienne. [*Looks at drinks.*]
TERRY: Can I get you something? There's gin. Sherry. Vodka.
ADRIENNE: Gin.
TERRY: I'll have a drop myself. Though I'm not very fond. [*Goes to sideboard, familiarly, and pours drink.*] Have you arrived today?

87

ADRIENNE: Yes. [*Glances up.*] I've just been resting.

TERRY: Here. Sit down. [*Takes her drink.*]

ADRIENNE: Thanks. [*Seated: feels around.*] I've left my bag upstairs. Have you got a cigarette?

TERRY: I don't smoke.

> [*As* ADRIENNE *makes to rise.*]

Here. I'll get you one. There's some in the kitchen. [*Goes.*

> ADRIENNE *covers her face a moment: hunches shoulders: endeavours to pull herself together.*
>
> *A moment later* TERRY *comes in.*]

Is that your trunk?

ADRIENNE: Yes.

TERRY: Nearly fell over it when I arrived.

ADRIENNE: There are a lot of people in this house.

TERRY: Yes.

ADRIENNE: Do you live here?

TERRY: No.

ADRIENNE: Does anyone live here, apart from Carol and Tom?

TERRY: Not permanently. People come in from time to time.

ADRIENNE: What do you do?

TERRY: I'm a teacher.

ADRIENNE: What do you teach? [*Lighting cigarette with great relief.*]

TERRY: Geography.

ADRIENNE: How long have you known Carol?

TERRY: About three years.

ADRIENNE: Are you a friend of hers or Tom's?

TERRY [*pause: genial*]: Both, I think.

ADRIENNE: Do you live in the town?

TERRY: Just outside.

> [ADRIENNE *smokes with relief for a moment: drinks.*]

ACT TWO

ADRIENNE: I'm sorry. I'm just coming awake. Train journeys devastate me. I hate travelling.

TERRY: Have you come far?

ADRIENNE: Fairly. [Sees feet.] I've come down without my shoes.

TERRY: That's all right. That's perfectly all right. Things are very informal here.

ADRIENNE: It's as if everybody owns it.

TERRY [watches her a moment. Then]: Would you like another drink?

ADRIENNE: I wouldn't mind.

TERRY: I'm more a whisky man myself. [Takes glass from her and goes to sideboard.] That's why Carol's out. Though she may have been detained by More. Once Maureen gets talking there's no stopping her. [Pauses.] Can't hear her. You can usually hear her voice through the wall. [Takes glass back to ADRIENNE.]

ADRIENNE: Thank you.

TERRY: You're married, too.

ADRIENNE: I have been.

TERRY: Oh.

ADRIENNE: And you?

TERRY [shakes head decisively]: I've more to do.

ADRIENNE: Such as?

TERRY [waits]: I want to think. I like to prepare things. [Suddenly] You come by train?

ADRIENNE: Yes.

TERRY: Did you notice the landscape when you came out of the tunnel?

ADRIENNE: Tunnel?

TERRY: There's a tunnel about two miles from here.

ADRIENNE: I must have been asleep. No. I woke up. The sound changed. I must have woken up just as we came out of it.

TERRY: Did you look out of the window?

ADRIENNE [*intrigued*]: I think so.

TERRY: The train comes through the southern edge of the valley: it runs in a cutting for about a hundred yards then suddenly emerges onto a high embankment. If you look to the left you can see Menstone Castle – a sort of mound like an inverted Christmas pudding.

ADRIENNE: I must have been looking the other way.

TERRY: Immediately below you is the river. It comes down through a gorge to the west and winds its way slowly towards the town. Now: the valley floor itself is very broad and flat. Do you know what it once was?

ADRIENNE: No. [*Shakes her head.*]

TERRY: A lake. In neolithic times. After the last ice-age, ten thousand years ago, a lake occupied the valley where the railway crosses. It's why the valley floor's so flat. And just below the town, where the river tumbles over rocks and crosses a weir, is the outlet from the lake which the river cut.

ADRIENNE: I see.

TERRY: Just below the castle: in fact, just below the cutting, is a broad footpath that crosses the fields – you can see it from here: it follows the contour of the valley side. Now that footpath marks the shore of the lake. If I took you to one of the upstairs windows, on a clear day, at the front, I could show you – where we are at the present – is just above the northern shore. Where Gold Cross Avenue now stands, immediately on the slope below us, in one or two of the gardens you can still see the traces of sand and grit: made by the water lapping up against the bank.

ADRIENNE: That's extraordinary. How did you find it out?

TERRY: I like thinking about the past. Above all, I like to see how the present grows out of the past: how everything

that happens now is a consequence of things that happened before: and similarly what happens now will shape
the things that happen in the future.

ADRIENNE: I see.

TERRY: If, for instance, you were to go along that footpath
you'd see that one side of the path is formed by a bank:
it rises about eight feet along one side. Now that, in fact,
is the bank of the neolithic lake: the footpath itself, along
which people, sometimes whole families, take a Sunday
walk, is the shore of the lake, the beach. You can still see
its configuration in the landscape. It shapes and directs
our lives in ways which, at first, we can't imagine.

ADRIENNE: Yes.

TERRY: I've found flints there: buried in the bank. Tiny bits
of stone. It must have been the spot where the neolithic
people came to fish. There are one or two bones shaped
as hooks. They're in the museum. But the pieces I found,
quite clearly, are arrow-heads. It's strange: where we're
sitting now, ten thousand years ago, naked or half-naked
men may well have been crouching, looking over the
waters of the lake at the fires glinting on the other side.
[Pause.] You're tired.

   [ADRIENNE brushes her hand aimlessly through her hair:
   takes her drink: she's finished it.]

Shall I get you another?

ADRIENNE: I wouldn't mind.

TERRY [gets up: takes her glass]: Do you take drugs?

ADRIENNE: What?

TERRY: Your pupils are dilated.

ADRIENNE: I have a . . . sedative.

TERRY: Are you under doctor's orders?

ADRIENNE: No.

TERRY: I like to ask about everything. [Has gone to pour her
drink.] It's why I come here as a matter of fact.

ADRIENNE: Why?

TERRY: It's so different.

ADRIENNE: What's so different?

TERRY: Carol. Tom. *Beryl.* Jo.

ADRIENNE: Where are they, as a matter of fact?

TERRY: Tom'll be at the boozer. He'd spend all day there if he got the chance. Not for the drinking. Dominoes is his present hobby. Beryl and Jo are upstairs.

ADRIENNE [*looks up*]: I thought I heard someone in the bathroom.

TERRY: They're an extraordinary couple. I've never met anyone like them. You've met them?

ADRIENNE: Yes. [*Takes drink: looks overhead again.* TERRY *settles himself in his chair again: relaxed, legs stretched out before him, hands in his lap.*]

TERRY: I've had a relatively sheltered life. An only child. Education was my parents' holy sepulchre. I wasn't very good: conscientious, yes. But brilliant, no. It's what *isn't* written in books, and what *isn't* taught, that's always fascinated me. Are you coming to live here permanently?

ADRIENNE: Why do you ask?

TERRY: I wondered. [*Pause.*]

ADRIENNE: There are several projects I have on hand. There were just a few days I thought I could get away. I haven't seen Carol . . . since she was almost a girl. I thought the opportunity might not come again.

TERRY: Your parents are dead?

ADRIENNE: Yes.

TERRY: So are mine. I don't miss them very much. I *loved* them very much, although I never believed in their views – they were very conservative and quite blind to the changes taking place around them. Anything I said they tended to dismiss, and were appalled when I finally went into teaching. That's only a stop–gap. I enjoy it still: but it won't detain me very long. I haven't found my focus yet.

ADRIENNE: Perhaps you're religious.

TERRY: I thought so for a time. I'm never sure what religious means. If I could define it — like Christianity — I don't think I'd want to believe it at all. Christ made one or two crucial errors. I'd say he was part of an evolving consciousness: I think that's how modern psychology would describe it: not as a fixed point of reference, but as something evolving which, in many ways, we've already discarded.

ADRIENNE: I've . . . [*Brushes her hand through her hair, looking round.*] seem to have left my bag upstairs.

TERRY: Here . . . [*Offers another cigarette: lights it for her.*] In prayer one's talking to oneself. To those parts of oneself which are inaccessible in everyday life. But who would ascribe — who needs to ascribe — those obscure parts of oneself to God? I'm sure they're in *us* and have no extraterrestrial significance.

ADRIENNE: It doesn't really matter, does it?

TERRY: Doesn't it?

ADRIENNE: If they're there. It's irrelevant to examine why there're there or what.

TERRY: I like to get to the root of everything. There *is* a root to everything. For instance: the world came out of nothing — a fact like that, by calculation, can't be true. Nothing is as impossible to imagine as a new colour. Something has always been there: something always will be there. [*Watches her a moment.*] When I have a personal problem . . . [*Pauses, suddenly: listens as if to a sound off.*] particularly one that gets me down, I go for a walk, or I stand at my window, and I look out towards the town. I look at the configuration of that now invisible lake, and I think, 'Ten thousand years ago this place wasn't even here: I wasn't here: this problem wasn't here. In another ten thousand years it's not unlikely it won't be here again: I won't be here. Whatever I was will be a handful of dust, a number of ill-assorted chemicals. In God knows how many aeons of time after that the earth itself won't even be here: what price our unhappiness – what price our problems then?' [*Laughs.*] An envelope of gas and debris slowly swirling round the sun.

ADRIENNE [*pause*]: Pain is still pain. An hour is still an hour. Unhappiness is still unhappiness even knowing that death will bring it to an end.

    [TERRY *gazes at her.* ADRIENNE *looks round blindly.*]

TERRY: Here. [*Takes out his handkerchief.*] Have mine. [*Gives it her.*]

ADRIENNE: It's nothing. [*Wipes eyes, briefly.*]

TERRY: I don't know you. Perhaps because of that you could tell me about it.

ADRIENNE: There's nothing to tell. [*Hands handkerchief back: gets another cigarette, briskly.*]

TERRY: Isn't there?

ADRIENNE: Nothing.

TERRY: Ask me anything about myself. Anything at all.

ADRIENNE: How old are you?

TERRY: Twenty-three.

ADRIENNE: Are you in love with Carol?

TERRY: Good lord, no.

ADRIENNE: What about the other two?

TERRY: Good lord! [*Laughs.*]

ADRIENNE: I don't understand this place.

TERRY: What? [*Laughs again.*]

ADRIENNE [*brushes her hand through her hair*]: This coming in and out: this living in one another's pocket.

TERRY: Hasn't Carol told you about this place?

ADRIENNE: What?

94

ACT TWO

[*Hall door opens:* JOANNA *comes in, fresh from bath.*]

JOANNA: God. Give me a drink. What're you having? [*To* TERRY]

TERRY: There's no Scotch.

JOANNA [*to* ADRIENNE]: Did you have a sleep?

ADRIENNE: Yes.

JOANNA [*to* TERRY *who has gone to drinks and holds up bottle*]: That'll do dandy.

TERRY: Adrienne was wondering what you girls get up to.

JOANNA: I wonder myself. Don't dilute it, my dear. It's not the quantity it's the quality that counts. Is Carol in?

TERRY: She's out.

JOANNA: I hope we didn't disturb you.

ADRIENNE: No.

JOANNA: My tummy is giving me the absolute jip. I've felt absolutely awful since I got up this morning. *And* I've had nothing to eat all day.

TERRY: You could do with losing something in any case.

JOANNA: On top of which that bath is far too small.

TERRY: It's regulation for a council house.

JOANNA: You can't lie down in it without some part of you above the water.

TERRY: Quite a problem I should think with you.

JOANNA [*to* ADRIENNE]: He comes here to make the jokes. He is the comedian of the establishment.

TERRY: I wish I were.

JOANNA: Has he told you about his history?

ADRIENNE: No.

TERRY: Geography is what I've been on about. Jo has no interest in anything that doesn't involve eating.

JOANNA [*consuming drink*]: I needed that. Got a terrible thirst. Kippers are full of salt, and fatty. Do you know how many calories one kipper is?

TERRY: Large or small?

95

JOANNA: Three hundred and eighty. That's as much as three and a half whole slices of bread.

TERRY: I don't know why she watches her figure: it's the nicest figure I know.

JOANNA: How long are you staying?

TERRY: I was going early. I don't mind waiting.

JOANNA: I should come up now. I'm going home early. Alex is in a terrible rage: he hates me to be ill or indisposed in the slightest way. [*To* ADRIENNE] My husband. [*Goes.*]

TERRY [*to* ADRIENNE]: I may see you later.

ADRIENNE: What?

> [TERRY *glances at her a moment: hesitates, then goes.*
>
> ADRIENNE, *alone, looks round the room: gets up: examines the papers and magazines. Looks round: crosses to the sideboard: opens cupboards, drawers: curiosity unsatisfied, frustrated, she pours another drink: holds her head.*
>
> *Door opens.*
>
> CRAWFORD *comes in: he's dressed in a policeman's uniform, although at the moment he's only got on the trousers, the braces, and the blue shirt, its collar undone. He's in his socks and carries his shoes and tie: a large, burly man, forty-two to -five.*]

CRAWFORD: Who are you?

ADRIENNE: I'm Adrienne.

CRAWFORD: I haven't seen you before.

ADRIENNE: I'm Carol's sister.

CRAWFORD: I didn't know she had one.

ADRIENNE: I arrived today.

CRAWFORD: Is she around?

ADRIENNE: No.

CRAWFORD: There's a can of beer in the fridge. Would you get us one?

ADRIENNE: Where is it?

CRAWFORD [*looks up, puzzled*]: In the kitchen.

ADRIENNE: Right.

CRAWFORD: Was that Terry on the stairs?

ADRIENNE: I think so.

CRAWFORD: Right.

> [ADRIENNE *pauses; then goes.*
>
> CRAWFORD *stoops to his shoes: groans, pulls them on.*]

Jesus. [*Struggles: belches.*] God. [*Gets last shoe on.*
Door opens. ADRIENNE *comes in with can of beer.*]
Where's the glass?

ADRIENNE: It'll be in the cupboard.

CRAWFORD: Right. [*Assumes she will get it: stoops to knot shoe.*

> ADRIENNE *hesitates, then goes to sideboard cupboard: gets out glass.*]

Been looking forward to this all day. Came off duty what? Two hours ago. What time is it?

ADRIENNE: About nine o'clock.

CRAWFORD: Get home for ten.

ADRIENNE: What . . . (are you?)

CRAWFORD: Cracker.

> [*Puts out his hand without getting up:* ADRIENNE *shakes it.*]

Crawford. Hence pseudo-name: Cracker. Cracker. First name Gordon. Gordon Crawford. Beryl's in the bathroom. These your fags?

ADRIENNE: No.

CRAWFORD: Adrienne. [*Getting cigarette.*] Don't think I've heard of you. This beer hasn't been in the fridge that long. Let's think. Adrienne. I should know your name.

ADRIENNE: I don't think so.

CRAWFORD: I've automatic recall. Can recall any fact I've ever been told. That was Jo, then, was it?

ADRIENNE: Yes.

CRAWFORD: How long are you staying?

ADRIENNE: I don't know.

CRAWFORD: What's the matter?

ADRIENNE: What?

CRAWFORD: Why are you cringing?

ADRIENNE: I didn't know I was.

CRAWFORD: I've telepathic instincts. [*Belches.*] I'm on your wavelength. I can tell you – if I concentrate – what you're thinking. Don't move. [*Covers his eyes with his hand: belches once again.*] You're thinking . . . [*Pause: concentrates: finally looks up.*] I don't think you like me very much. This your glass?

ADRIENNE: No.

CRAWFORD: Been talking to Terry?

ADRIENNE: Yes.

CRAWFORD: Is Tom in?

ADRIENNE: I don't think so.

CRAWFORD: Mrs Donaldson about?

ADRIENNE: No.

CRAWFORD: You don't have much conversation do you? [*Watches her a moment.*] I'm not on duty, you know.

ADRIENNE: No.

CRAWFORD: It's only a uniform. [*Indicates his chest.*] There's a real flesh-and-blood person under this.

[ADRIENNE *doesn't answer.*]

Here. [*Gets up, intrigued.*] You're frightened of me.

ADRIENNE: No.

CRAWFORD: What's up, then?

ADRIENNE: Nothing.

CRAWFORD: You can tell me. If I could have a penny for every life-story told me by a woman I'd be the richest man in town. Married?

ADRIENNE: No.

CRAWFORD: Not married. Wears ring. Divorced. Thirty:

98

could be older. No children: otherwise would be here.
Nervous temperament. Criminal record: doubtful. I'm
not here to frighten you. Carol'll laugh at this, I can tell
you that.

ADRIENNE: I'm not frightened.

CRAWFORD: Do you want a fag?

ADRIENNE: I wouldn't mind.

[CRAWFORD *gets her one: lights it for her.*]

CRAWFORD: You're not very much like your sister.

ADRIENNE: No.

CRAWFORD: I'm a law-and-order man. Public law and
public order. What goes on in private is very much your
own affair.

ADRIENNE: Do you live here?

CRAWFORD: I'm married. I've a wife and two children.
Let's see. I go back on duty in about twelve hours. Put
your feet up. Have a drink.

ADRIENNE: I've had one.

CRAWFORD: There's nothing goes on in here that doesn't
go on anywhere else. [*Indicates his chest.*] I'm not super-
human. I'm your average law-abiding citizen.

ADRIENNE: Yes.

CRAWFORD: When were you married?

ADRIENNE: Six years ago.

CRAWFORD: Broke up recent.

ADRIENNE: Two years ago.

CRAWFORD: Should have children. Children cement a
marriage.

ADRIENNE: I had a child.

CRAWFORD: Had you?

ADRIENNE: At least I had a miscarriage. It was quite a
beautiful baby. It was almost seven months.

CRAWFORD: Beautiful at that age?

ADRIENNE: The doctor told me that it was.

CRAWFORD: Husband disappointed?

ADRIENNE: Not really.

CRAWFORD: Selfish bastard.

ADRIENNE: Was he?

CRAWFORD: You're getting very cool. [*Listens.*] That's Terry. He'll be here till dawn. Has more theories about more things than anyone I could mention. Did he tell you about his dog?

ADRIENNE: No.

CRAWFORD: What did he talk about?

ADRIENNE: A lake.

CRAWFORD: What lake?

ADRIENNE: It existed here. I think he said ten thousand years ago.

CRAWFORD: He's the most curious bastard I've ever known. Mention some subject that nobody's ever heard of and he'll come up with an answer.

ADRIENNE: What is this house?

CRAWFORD: What?

ADRIENNE: What is it? What goes on upstairs?

CRAWFORD: Thy sister hasn't told you?

ADRIENNE: I don't know. [*Holds head.*] You better tell me.

CRAWFORD: Nay, love. Thy's in a hell of a state. [*Puts his arm about her.*]

ADRIENNE: Don't touch me!

CRAWFORD: Sithee: I'm not going to eat you. I'll take this shirt off, if you like. A policeman's uniform has a very funny effect upon a lot of people. It's something to do with their childhood.

ADRIENNE: Just leave me alone! [*Wrenches herself away as the door from the hall opens.*

BERYL comes in: she wears a long dressing-gown and is smoking.]

BERYL: You still here?

CRAWFORD: I was having a drink.

BERYL: Where's your jacket?

CRAWFORD: I left it upstairs.

BERYL: If More isn't here I'll get something to eat. Do you want something, do you?

CRAWFORD: I wouldn't mind a sandwich if thy's getting one.

BERYL: Right. [*Pause: to* ADRIENNE] Do you want anything, love?

ADRIENNE: No thanks.

[BERYL *glances at* CRAWFORD: *goes.*
Composing herself.]

When it was born the doctor, afterwards, said he wished he'd allowed me to see it.

CRAWFORD: This baby of yours.

ADRIENNE: It was four years ago. We had its name down for a school. At least, my husband had. We'd have broken up in any case. I think if a child comes from a broken home it doesn't stand much chance with anything.

CRAWFORD: I think background's over-rated myself. Terry always goes on about that.

ADRIENNE: I . . . [*Gestures round with arm.*] had an opportunity which I had to forgo because of it.

CRAWFORD: It'll always come again.

ADRIENNE: Will it?

CRAWFORD: Everything comes in threes. Trouble, sorrow, joy and wealth.

ADRIENNE: That's four things.

CRAWFORD: Sorrow, joy and wealth. Three of each makes nine. You have a sensitive temperament. You shouldn't let these things get you down.

ADRIENNE: Yes.

CRAWFORD: Don't let them get on top. They're all rough 'uns in this house. Nice on top, but rough beneath. I know. I'm not above mixing it myself. Not with everybody, mind. In a place like this, sensitivity, tha knows, goes by the board.

ADRIENNE: When I lived at home . . . it was a place very much like this. Not as neat. It had no . . . vision. It had no dreams. And what thoughts it did have were common and cheap. I can't describe what it was like. I lavished all my love on Carol: I thought, 'I'll get her out of a place like this.' I went away to make my fortune. It was there: oh, it was so nearly there. I could have touched it . . . [*Pushes back her hair.*] Just when I was free, just when I felt it was taking off . . . I had a baby.

CRAWFORD [*pause. Then*]: You should have aborted it.

ADRIENNE: I couldn't kill a living thing.

CRAWFORD: It's not living.

ADRIENNE: Isn't it?

CRAWFORD: Not for a while. Tha's two or three months you know when tha could have got rid of it.

ADRIENNE: It's extraordinary . . . it's what my husband said . . . I thought I should save it . . . I thought, you see, it might be like Jesus.

[CRAWFORD *gazes at her.*]

ADRIENNE: I said, 'Suppose it's like the Second Coming.'

CRAWFORD [*pause*]: I don't understand.

ADRIENNE: Suppose it was Christ. Suppose Mary had had a child: suppose the second Mary had had an abortion.

CRAWFORD: I see what you mean. We're all waiting here for a new Messiah and the bastards went and aborted him. That's like one of Terry's thoughts is that: only he's not religious like me. You're religious. You could have had another.

ADRIENNE: I didn't want another. [*Turns away.*] I didn't really want one at all. It's not necessary today, for a woman to fulfil herself. I could have fulfilled myself in other ways. Like a man. Not like a man. Like a poet. I could have salvaged something. My father was always in debt. Carol may have told you. He had such dreams – building an empire, he once described it. He had a shop: it went bankrupt. He had a small-holding: it became a farm before we'd been there a week. He had no idea of growth: he built up a factory: he started so many businesses I don't think if you asked me I could remember half of them. He had wonderful schemes for so many things. It was all in his head: not one of them ever came to anything. And whenever he had any money, whenever he had any single stroke of luck he let my mother spend it. He wanted her to feel grand: he wanted her to feel he'd really succeeded. He had . . . such courage. Such belief: such conviction. Nothing, not even all these failures, got him down: ruin in one thing was merely the prelude to him taking up with something else. I loved him: I couldn't stand his life. I couldn't stand the failure with which he surrounded himself. I couldn't see him measure his dreams in my mother's eyes, only to see them fade again. He turned her into a queen for twenty-four hours. Twenty-four hours: that's how long anything ever lasted. [*Turns aside.*

Door has opened from hall.

CAROL *stands there: dressed in outdoor coat and hat: she has three bottles wrapped in paper.*

CRAWFORD *looks up at her.*

Then, gazing in from the door:]

CAROL: What is it?

ADRIENNE: I . . . woke up. I heard a noise in the bathroom.

CAROL: I've just been down to the shops. I looked in your room: you were sound asleep.

ADRIENNE: It must have been the bathroom. I've been

talking to this gentleman here. [*Turns away: gets cigarette.*]
I'll just go up and get my shoes. [*Goes.*]

CAROL: Have you upset her?

CRAWFORD: Not me, love. I just came in a few minutes since.

CAROL: What have you told her?

CRAWFORD: I've told her nothing. She seems to know naught about anything.

CAROL: She's my sister.

CRAWFORD: I've discovered that.

> [CAROL *takes bottles to the sideboard: puts them down: unbuttons her coat, thoughtful.*
> CRAWFORD *moves over to her quickly to help her off with it.*]

She wa' going on about this baby.

CAROL: What baby?

CRAWFORD: She had one. Still–born. Almost four year ago. Ruined her career, she said.

CAROL: Could you hang it up?

CRAWFORD: Right.

> [*As he goes to hall door the kitchen door opens and* BERYL *comes in with plate of sandwiches: she's still smoking.*
> CRAWFORD *takes* CAROL's *coat out to the hall.*]

CAROL: Have you been talking to Adrienne?

BERYL: When, love? I've been upstairs.

CAROL: Is Terry still here?

BERYL: He's upstairs now.

> [CAROL *sits.*]

Where's More?

CAROL: She's decorating a cake.

BERYL: What for?

CAROL: For a surprise. For a *homecoming*.

BERYL: I'm not complaining.

CAROL: It sounds just a bit like it, love, to me.

[CRAWFORD *comes back in from hall: doesn't say anything: he's brought his police jacket and is pulling it on.*]

BERYL: He looks well: coming here in his uniform.

CAROL: I don't mind him coming with his uniform.

CRAWFORD: Lends respectability, I can tell you that.

BERYL: Something we're not short of.

CRAWFORD: This my sandwich?

BERYL: That's right.

CRAWFORD: Drop of the hard stuff, have we? [*Goes to sideboard.*]

CAROL: It's what I went out to buy. To celebrate.

CRAWFORD [*chewing*]: What you celebrating, love?

BERYL: She's celebrating her sister coming.

CRAWFORD: If she's living in a knocking-shop, I think somebody ought to tell her.

CAROL: It's not a knocking-shop.

CRAWFORD: It is in my book. And my book, I ought to tell you, is the law's.

CAROL: You're a hypocrite and a bloody fool.

CRAWFORD: Now. Now. Where's thy husband? I usually have time for a game of rummy.

CAROL: He's down at the pub. I asked him to come up: he said he wouldn't.

BERYL: She'll be all right, you know.

CAROL: What?

BERYL: She'll only be here a couple of days.

CAROL: Yes.

BERYL: Do you mind her coming?

CAROL: I hadn't really thought of it. She was *due* tomorrow. I hadn't made any appointments then.

BERYL: Office in the morning. I'm thinking of giving it up.

CRAWFORD: You can't make a living at this game. Not in a place like this.

BERYL: I don't have to stay in this place, do I?

[CAROL *gazes up, wondering whether to go upstairs.*]
I should leave her for a bit, love. She'll come down when she's ready.

CAROL: She was such a dreamer. She used to dream such wonderful things. I always felt guilty I couldn't dream them as well: she really wanted to excel: she really wanted to achieve things. I think I was the only practical one in the family. My father, my mother: she's inherited all their faults. I seem to have inherited all their virtues: nothing ever gets me down even when I think it should. *She* might get me down. Perhaps this once I'll have a taste of what it's really like.

[*Door opens: they all look up.*

TERRY *comes in from hall, dressed as before.*]

CRAWFORD: That wa' quick.

TERRY: What're you drinking?

CRAWFORD: I'm having a sandwich. [*Has already left the sideboard with a whisky, diluted, and is eating once again.*]

TERRY: Owt going?

CAROL: There's some whisky. I've just brought it in.

TERRY: Any more coming in tonight?

CAROL: Don't know.

BERYL: *I've* got nobody. Three in one evening is quite enough.

CRAWFORD: Money thy earns tha mu'n buy a place of your own.

BERYL: I don't need a place of my own.

TERRY: I've just been opening your sister's trunk.

CAROL: What?

TERRY: She asked me to take it upstairs.

[CRAWFORD *laughs.*]

I said later. I opened it for her.

CAROL: Has she come down?

106

TERRY: She went back up. [*To* BERYL] I wouldn't mind a drink if you're pouring out.

CRAWFORD: Fancy a hand at rummy?

TERRY: No thanks.

CRAWFORD: I'll have another beer.

CAROL: I'll get it. [*Goes out through kitchen door.*]

CRAWFORD: She'll sneak up. See if her sister's all right. I'll give you a lift later if tha's off back home.

TERRY: Right.

CRAWFORD: Make it more convivial. More, tha knows, like a family party.

[*JOANNA comes in from hall, dressed as before.*]

JOANNA: Come to arrest us, sergeant? [*Goes to sideboard: pours drink.*]

CRAWFORD: I'll arrest you any time you like.

JOANNA: Any more at the station like you?

CRAWFORD: There's one or two.

JOANNA: Be having us shut up before we know where we are.

CRAWFORD: I know the highways and byways of the law blindfold. And by that I meant the *back*-highways and the *back*-byways: those gaps that civilians like you know naught about.

JOANNA: You're a disgrace to your profession.

CRAWFORD [*to* BERYL]: Ever thought of joining, have you?

BERYL: It depends what sort of skills they want.

CRAWFORD: You could keep up the morale, tha knows, in the cells.

BERYL: I keep it up here: and that, I can tell you, is hard enough.

CRAWFORD: Not hard enough for me, my love. [*Embraces her.*] We could have you out as a decoy, you know. Just look at this.

[*The door from the kitchen has opened.*]

TOM *comes in, open jacket and open-necked shirt: three bottles wrapped in paper in his arms.*]

TOM: She's not gone and bloody well bought three, has she? I *said* I'd get them. That's six. [*Sets bottles down on the sideboard.*] The arrangements in this house take some beating.

CRAWFORD: Fancy gin-rummy, Tom?

TOM: I fancy summat to eat. Is Maureen here?

BERYL: She's decorating a cake.

TOM: What for?

BERYL: Your sister-in-law's homecoming.

TOM: It's no bloody home *she's* coming to: this is strictly a temporary visit. I know that sort.

TERRY: What sort is she?

TOM: A sponger.

JOANNA: He'd know about that, of course, himself.

BERYL: What's that mean, for Christ's sake?

JOANNA: They don't call him the unemployment king for nothing.

BERYL: He employs you.

JOANNA: I employ him.

BERYL: Do you?

TOM: I employ *all* of you: so shut your mouth. *He* takes his rake-off. [CRAWFORD] So does she. [JOANNA]

BERYL: What about me, sweetheart? [*Arm round him: winks at others.*]

TOM [*to* CRAWFORD]: What's she charge?

CRAWFORD: Tha mu'n bloody ask her. Are you sure you wouldn't like a game o' rummy?

TOM: I broke up a game of rummy to come up here. She asked me to bring it up: said it was urgent. F'und she's bought three already.

[CAROL *comes in from hall: carries can of beer.*]

BERYL: All right, is she?

CAROL [*casually*]: I knocked at her door. She said so. [*Hands can to* CRAWFORD.] You're back. [*To* TOM.]

TOM: I've brought three, an' all.

CAROL: You said you hadn't got time.

TOM: I f'und the time.

CAROL: Pity you couldn't have found it sooner.

TOM: If I'd known you were buying it then I wouldn't.

CAROL: If I'd known you were buying it then I wouldn't.

TERRY: Since you've *both* bought some we can all have a drink.

JOANNA: I've had mine.

BERYL: And mine.

CRAWFORD: Got mine.

TERRY: I'll have another.

TOM: I'll have one.

JOANNA [*to* CAROL]: Here's to it, love.

CRAWFORD: Here's to it.

[BERYL *raises her glass, too.*]

TOM: Welcome home! [*Holds up glass, saluting towards ceiling. They laugh, but for* CAROL: *as they toast and raise their glasses: a knock on the kitchen door: it opens.*

MRS DONALDSON *comes in.*]

MRS DONALDSON: Is everyone ready, then?

TOM: What for?

MRS DONALDSON [*to* CAROL]: Shall I bring it in?

CAROL: She isn't down, love.

CRAWFORD: She has been down, but she's gone back up.

[*Laughter.*]

CAROL: I should bring it in, love, in any case.

MRS DONALDSON [*looks round at them. Then*]: Right. [*Goes.*]

CRAWFORD: What's she gotten?

JOANNA: Wouldn't you be surprised.

CAROL: Can you hold the door?

[TERRY *goes to the kitchen door as it half-opens and closes again to a cry: holds it open: gestures:*

MRS DONALDSON *comes in with an iced cake held before her. On top are four candles.*]

TOM: Whose birthday is it?

MRS DONALDSON: Nobody's birthday. Four candles is all I had. [*To* CAROL] At such short notice.

TERRY: It looks very beautiful, Mrs Donaldson.

MRS DONALDSON [*to* CAROL]: Will she come down, do you think, to see it?

CRAWFORD: I've never seen wedding cake in a knocking-shop afore.

MRS DONALDSON: It's not a wedding cake. It's a fruit cake with marzipan and almond icing.

BERYL: Did you bake it yourself, then, More?

MRS DONALDSON: I bought it. I hadn't time to prepare it. [*To* CAROL] I thought you'd appreciate it, love.

CRAWFORD: Tha'd better bring down the guest of honour. [*Stands with his arm round* JOANNA.]

CAROL [*standing quickly*]: I'll fetch her.

TERRY: I don't mind going. Which room is it?

CRAWFORD: *And* come down, tha knows.

CAROL: It's the back bedroom.

TERRY: Right. [*Goes out through hall door.*]

MRS DONALDSON: Well. [*Looks round at them: looks at the cake.*] If I'd had that bit longer. If I'd had some *notice*.

CAROL: I think you've said all that before.

MRS DONALDSON: I like to be of some value, love. [*Turns away: weeps: the others are evidently familiar with her manner.*]

CAROL: You are a lot of value.

MRS DONALDSON [*to others*]: I keep this place a picture. [*To* CAROL] It's not fair that someone should come and spoil it.

CAROL: No one's come and spoilt it.

MRS DONALDSON [to others]: I have no one. Since my husband died I've tried to make a go of things.

JOANNA: Have a drop of something, More.

MRS DONALDSON: Well, if you're all having something.

CRAWFORD: I'll get it. [Goes to sideboard, familiar with what she'll drink.]

MRS DONALDSON: I don't give in to feeling much.

CAROL: No.

MRS DONALDSON: If I'd had children of my own things might be different. I treat Carol as my daughter: I love her just as much.

TOM: We know that, Mother. And we're very proud of you. [Puts his arm round her and kisses her cheek.]

TERRY [entering from hall]: I didn't know there was a lock on that bedroom door.

CAROL: There isn't.

TERRY: It wouldn't open.

TOM: She's wedged a chair under the handle. That's more thy sort of gambit, Cracker.

CRAWFORD: I'm off home, tha knows, if you start to quarrel. I come here to enjoy myself. I can have arguments at home. [To CAROL] Domestic squabbles should not intrude on business.

CAROL: They're not intruding. Since she came it's just that I don't know where I am. Is she coming down?

TERRY: She said so. [Picks up drink of his own.]

TOM: I should have stayed at the pub. I knew when I bought those three it was a mistake coming back.

CAROL: What did she sound like?

TERRY: She sounded all right.

CRAWFORD: She's been bloody upset, I can tell you that. I can read character like a book. Present any person to me and I can read off what they're thinking from looking at their faces. It's part of my training: it's also part of my natural equipment.

BERYL: I've *seen* his natural equipment and it's nothing to write home about.

CRAWFORD: What was that?

BERYL: Stuff like that you should keep under cover.

CRAWFORD [*fist*]: I'm not above pushing this right down your throat.

BERYL: It won't be the first thing he's pushed down there.

TERRY: Now, children. Now, comrades. Friends. This is not the occasion for an argument. As Cracker has rightly said: we can quarrel, all of us, as much as we like at home.

CRAWFORD: The more I see of her [BERYL] the more she gets like my wife.

BERYL: Your wife wouldn't even go to bed with you.

CRAWFORD: My wife goes to bed with me whenever I like. Two o'clock. Three o'clock. Any time I like. When a woman gets to a certain age, however, when a marriage gets to a certain age, a husband's sexual demands are not always welcome to a wife. She's even relieved if her husband can get satisfaction, *of that nature*, somewhere else. My wife's like that. She appreciates it. It's why, after all these years, we have a happy and a satisfactory marriage. It's why we have two happy sons: it's why I have a steady job and why I can do it to the very best of my ability. [*To* TERRY] Are you laughing at me?

TERRY: I'm not laughing.

CRAWFORD: That looks very much like a laugh to me.

TERRY: I'm wincing.

CRAWFORD: Why's he wincing?

TERRY: I wince. I often wince.

CRAWFORD: You ought to be frightened of me. You all

ought to be frightened. I could shop the bloody lot of you.

TOM: We could shop you, if it comes to that. *I* could shop you: *she* [BERYL] could shop you.

TERRY: We're held together, you see, like all the best social institutions, by our mutual dependency.

CRAWFORD: If anyone laughs at me you know what I do?

TERRY: No.

CRAWFORD: I stamp on their balls.

TERRY: How do you do that if they're standing up?

JOANNA: He only hits people who're lying down.

BERYL: He only screws people who're lying down.

CRAWFORD: I'll screw you, you little cunt! [*Leaps on her in fury.*

> BERYL *screams: is knocked into chair,* CRAWFORD *on top of her.*
>
> *Amidst her screams and* JOANNA's *and* TERRY's *attempts to restrain him:* 'I'll kill her!'
>
> ADRIENNE *enters from the hall.*]

CAROL: Cracker!

TERRY: Cracker.

> [CRAWFORD *gets up: turning.*]

JOANNA: The mad bastard: they'd only have a mad bastard like that in the police.

CRAWFORD: What?

JOANNA: Thug.

CRAWFORD [*to* JOANNA]: I'll deal with you later.

JOANNA: They'd only have morons like that in the bloody gestapo.

CAROL: Shut it. Shut your mouth at once.

> [ADRIENNE *stands in the door but has stepped in slightly: she wears a light but expensive and attractive dress: her hair is neat: she wears a necklace and carries a tiny bag clasped to her wrist.*]

That's beautiful. That looks so beautiful, love. [*Kisses her.*]

ADRIENNE: Thank you. [*She goes directly to the cake. Gazes at it.*] Did you make it, Mrs Donaldson?

MRS DONALDSON: I decorated it.

ADRIENNE [*to* CAROL]: I take it it is for us? Carol: shall we cut it together?

MRS DONALDSON: I've brought a knife on the tray.

ADRIENNE: We'll light the candles. We'll have a wish. We'll put out the lights. Everyone will be silent and close their eyes. Four candles . . .

MRS DONALDSON: That's all I had.

ADRIENNE: My child, you know, would be four this year. My career would have been four also . . .

TERRY: Here. I've got a match. [*Steps forward: lights candles.*]

ADRIENNE [*to* CRAWFORD]: Would you mind? The switch.

CRAWFORD: Right. [*Steps to the light-switch by the hall door.*]

ADRIENNE: Carol. It's like a birthday.

CAROL: Yes.

ADRIENNE: Or a wedding. Are you ready for your wish?

CAROL: Yes.

ADRIENNE: You must tell it to no one. No one must know. If no one knows it will always come true.

TERRY: Always?

[*The light goes out: room lit by the candles.*]

ADRIENNE: We'll blow together. Everyone, of course, must close their eyes. If anyone opens their eyes the wish will never come true.

[*They stoop to the cake: they blow together: the room is in darkness.*

After a moment:]

TOM: All right, for Christ's sake.

[*Light comes on.*

ADRIENNE *stands there a moment, as if caught by her feeling.*

CAROL *gazes at her. Then:*]

ADRIENNE: Right. [*She picks up the knife.*] Put your hand on mine: or should mine, do you think, be on yours? Mine on yours; the older covers and protects the younger.

CAROL: Yes.

ADRIENNE: Are you ready?

CAROL: Right.

[*They cut the cake together.*]

MRS DONALDSON: There are some plates on the side, you see.

ADRIENNE: Tom: could you fill the glasses, please.

[TOM *looks at her: hesitates: then does so.*]

ADRIENNE: Terry: would you pass round the plates?

TERRY: Right.

ADRIENNE: It's not often in life you have anything to celebrate: the prodigal's return: the family united: the discovery of friends . . . the feeling that life after all has got a purpose. [*To* JOANNA] Would you like a piece?

JOANNA: My stomach won't take it. Bartlett's, you see. It's one of Bartlett's. All the fruit has gone to the bottom.

MRS DONALDSON: They're the only bakers in town who do a cake like this. [*To* ADRIENNE] I didn't want a mass-produced one. It's individually baked.

BERYL: Individually baked and burned.

CRAWFORD: It's lovely. It's delicious.

BERYL: Don't you pass it to the ladies first?

CRAWFORD: I'm testing it. [*To* ADRIENNE] A policeman's privilege.

ADRIENNE: I shall propose a toast. [*To* TOM] If you'd allow me. [TERRY *has passed her a glass.*] Mrs Donaldson: if you could cut the remaining pieces. Has everyone got a glass?

CRAWFORD: We're all provided. We're all equipped.

ADRIENNE: I propose a toast . . . Not to lost dreams . . . not to faded hopes and ambitions . . . I should like to propose a toast to the present . . . [*To* TERRY] Whatever the past may have been . . . whatever the future may hold . . . to now. To a feeling that at last I have come amongst friends . . . to a feeling that at last I have found a home. To now . . . to all that the present holds for us . . . to us . . . to all of us, on this extraordinary and oh so lovely planet . . . [*To* TERRY] on the shores of this oh so ancient lake . . . to all of us . . . to now . . . to my sister Carol . . . to my dear, dear sister . . . whose rainbow I would have wished so much to have found for her . . . whose rainbow I would have found so long ago. To now, my dear: to all we might have missed and have now retrieved . . . to now.

[*They raise their glasses with varying degrees of doubt*: 'To Now.']

Do you have any music? We can have a dance. Anything, this evening, goes. This evening we shall remember for the rest of our lives . . . we shall refuse to let this place dictate to us. Life shall not form us . . . Terry . . . Carol . . . Mrs Donaldson . . . it shall not succeed in shaping us. To us!

[CAROL *turns on the gramophone.*

To TERRY] Would you care to dance? Would you care to forget the past, and its shaping of our present? Would you care to invest in now? Would you care to take me as I really am?

[TERRY *takes her hands.*

With style and grace, to the music, they begin to dance, the others standing back, clearing the furniture, to watch them: they watch with pleasure, surprise and admiration.

Light fades.]

ACT THREE

*The curtains on the windows are drawn: the room is half-dark,
with daylight outside.*

After a moment the door from the kitchen opens and MRS
DONALDSON *comes in. Goes to curtains: opens them.*

*The disarrangement of the furniture is revealed: chairs and
coffee table pushed back, cushions scattered, rug and carpet
rumpled: bottles, glasses, ash-trays, plates.*

*Starts tidying immediately, clearing and alternately pushing
furniture back into place.*

TERRY *comes in: shirtsleeves and trousers and tousled hair.*

TERRY [*looks at wrist-watch*]: Here. More: will you do me a
favour?

MRS DONALDSON: I've enough favours to do with this.

TERRY: Go down to the phone and ring up school. Tell 'em
I don't think I'll be in this morning. [*Sneezes.*] You could
say I've got a cold. [*Holds head.*]

MRS DONALDSON: It's not a cold you've got, young man.

TERRY: Will you? Will you? [*Endeavours to court her.*] Will
you do just one thing for me?

MRS DONALDSON: I'll go down when I've finished this.

TERRY [*looks round at room*]: What a mess. I've never seen it
as rough as this. [*Yawns.*] I'll give you a hand.

MRS DONALDSON: No thanks.

TERRY: Coffee or tea?

MRS DONALDSON: You'll find some coffee in the kitchen.

TERRY: Right. [*Yawns again: goes out to kitchen.*

   MRS DONALDSON *clears.*

Reappears.] Do you want a cup?

MRS DONALDSON: I didn't celebrate as much as you. In addition to which I've had a cup.

TERRY: Right. [*Goes.*

    MRS DONALDSON *pauses: picks up book of newspaper cuttings from the floor: pauses to read.*

    Kitchen door opens: TERRY *comes in with coffee.*]

MRS DONALDSON: Is this her husband?

TERRY [*looks at cuttings over her shoulder*]: Married I believe no longer. Owes everything to her, however.

MRS DONALDSON: Just look at that. A house. More like a palace.

TERRY: There's one other further on. [*Turns pages for her: doesn't find it.*] A yacht. More like the *Mauretania*. Has berths, she said, for twenty-five. God: I really enjoyed that. Not often have a fling like that.

    [*Door opens:* TOM *comes in: trousers, vest: from hall. Goes directly to drinks. None left of what he wants.*]

There's some coffee, Tom.

TOM: Is there. [*Goes out to kitchen.*]

MRS DONALDSON: *That* young man will not be fit to speak to anyone today.

TERRY: I admired your dancing.

MRS DONALDSON: Did you?

TERRY: Never knew you had such grace.

MRS DONALDSON: Never had the chance to show it.

TERRY: Care for a demonstration now? [*Arms out.*]

MRS DONALDSON [*on her way out with plates, glasses, bottles*]: Schooling is the thing you ought to be on about. [*Goes out to kitchen.*]

TERRY [*calling*]: That's why I want you to ring!

    [*Kitchen door opens immediately.*

    TOM *comes in: sets pot down. Searches round.*]

TOM: Any cigarettes?

TERRY: Here. [*Finds them for him.*]

TOM: What's she on about?

TERRY: Have to ring up school. Ill. [*Coughs.*]

TOM: Bloody good job is that. Day off whenever you like.

TERRY: Like yours.

TOM: What?

TERRY: Enjoy it? [*Indicates room: party.*]

TOM: All right. [*Sits, smoking, pot in hand.*]

TERRY: Up early.

TOM: Am I.

TERRY: Not that I'd know what time you normally rise.

TOM: That's right.

    [*Smokes:* TERRY *watches him. Finally:*]

TERRY: Heard the argument last night.

TOM: What argument.

TERRY: You and Carol. [*Laughs.*] Couldn't help but hear.
Nothing unusual, of course, in that.

TOM [*gazes at him for a moment. Then*]: All food you eat in
this house you have to pay for.

TERRY: That's right.

TOM: Bed as well.

TERRY: I'm not complaining.

TOM: You think you're so superior, don't you.

TERRY: I do not.

TOM: This educated look: this . . . facility with words.

TERRY: I'm not very facile at all. I admired your dancing,
by the way, last night.

TOM: Did you? I used to move like that when I played. I
had one thing that no one could ever take from me.
Know what it was? *Talent.* Finally, incontrovertibly, I
was screwed up by a woman.

    [MRS DONALDSON *comes in: brush, pan: from kitchen.*]
Clear it later.

MRS DONALDSON: I'm going to clear it now.

TOM [*gazes at her a moment. Then*]: Things from now on are going to be different.

TERRY: In what way?

TOM: Lots of ways. For one thing, I shall start again. Know how old I am? Twenty-nine. I've got four years still in me.

TERRY: What about all the booze?

TOM: What booze?

[TERRY *gestures round.*]

TOM: I could sink eleven pints on Friday and play a blinder on Saturday afternoon. I have the constitution: I have the strength: and that one thing that no one can take away.

TERRY: Motivation.

TOM: What?

TERRY: Motivation is the one thing no one can destroy.

TOM: A woman screwed me up. I gave her everything. I even got this house ahead of the list. A committee man was on the council. I bought her a car: television: there was nothing I didn't do for that woman.

MRS DONALDSON: You have a wonderful wife at present. It's things for her you ought to be doing.

TOM: You keep out of this.

MRS DONALDSON: I'll not keep out of it and see that wonderful woman abused.

TOM: She's a wonderful woman.

MRS DONALDSON: She's everything a man like you could possibly desire. [*To* TERRY] She's *educated* him to a better standard. She's picked him off the floor and set him on his feet again.

TOM: All right. All right. Go and shove that cleaner somewhere else.

MRS DONALDSON: I'll finish in here: *then* there are the beds to do.

TOM: Is Joanna here?

TERRY: That's right.

MRS DONALDSON: On top of which you couldn't even if you wanted kick a ball again . . . I hear you coughing. I hear you wheezing. Lack of exercise and drinking: walking to the pub and back is all the exercise that creature gets.

TOM: Things from now on are going to be different. I'm fit: I'm fitter now than I ever was.

MRS DONALDSON [tidying]: Fit to drop is all you are.

TOM: J was a professional footballer for over four years.

MRS DONALDSON: A professional drinker is far more like it.

TOM: I was a star. My wife screwed up my chance. There's nothing I wouldn't have done for her. I proved it to her again and again. I worshipped the ground that woman walked on.

MRS DONALDSON: Pity you didn't worship this and do a bit of scrubbing. [To TERRY] I was here. I saw it happen before my eyes. When Carol arrived she changed his life.

TOM [turning away]: Did Cracker go?

TERRY: He went home. I don't know whether he ever arrived. He's supposed to be at work this morning.

TOM: If he's directing traffic he'll be a delight to see. Do you know what he did once after a night spent here? Boarded a bus and arrested the driver. The funny thing was: it turned out the man's licence was out of date, and he'd been prosecuted for a driving offence which he'd omitted to declare on his application. Result: conviction. Cracker put it down to intuition: 'Show me a face and I can tell you what it's thinking.'

[They laugh together.

ADRIENNE enters.

The room now is almost tidy, with TERRY occasionally

drawing a piece of furniture into place round MRS DONALD-
SON's *cleaning.*

ADRIENNE *wears a light-coloured dress: fresh, alert, lively,
as if for a performance.*]

ADRIENNE: Morning!

TERRY: Good morning.

[TOM *turns away to take his mug.*]

ADRIENNE: Is that coffee I can smell, Mrs Donaldson?

MRS DONALDSON: It is. [*Waits*].

ADRIENNE: I'd love a cup. [*Goes to window: looks out.*] That
shore of the lake: I can almost hear the water lapping!

[MRS DONALDSON *watches her: glances at the others: goes
out to kitchen.*]

TOM: Were you in the bathroom when I knocked just now?

ADRIENNE: I was.

TOM: You realize you've taken all the hot water.

ADRIENNE: It'll soon heat up.

TOM: That's an immersion. It all costs money. When the
fire isn't lit it costs a bomb.

ADRIENNE: I'll pay for it.

TOM: What.

ADRIENNE: Tell me how much it costs.

TERRY: I'll run up if it's free, and have a wash. [TERRY *nods
at* ADRIENNE *pleasantly: goes out through hall door.
Heard off:*] Mrs Donaldson? Can you go now and ring
them for me?

MRS DONALDSON [*Off*]: I can *not*. [*Enters from kitchen with
coffee and bowl.*] There's the coffee. The milk is in. And
there's the sugar.

ADRIENNE: You're very kind. I never thanked you for the
cake last night.

MRS DONALDSON: It was all in the way of service. [*Goes.*]

ADRIENNE [*looks round, freshly*]: Well.

[*Picks up coffee:* TOM *affects not to be aware of her.*]

Is Carol up?

TOM: I've no idea.

ADRIENNE: Are these your cigarettes?

TOM: That's right.

ADRIENNE: Do you mind if I have one?

TOM: Help yourself.

[ADRIENNE *takes one: looks round for a light:* TOM *doesn't offer her one. She picks up a lighter herself.*]

People pay for the things they use round here.

ADRIENNE: Do they?

TOM: I've met your type, you know, before.

ADRIENNE: What type?

TOM: Your type. What I say in this house goes. I own this house. Everything in here is mine. My wife was like you. My first wife: she thought she had it all worked out.

ADRIENNE: I don't know what you mean.

TOM: Climb in the saddle: ride to posterity on my back. I give no one a ride.

ADRIENNE: I'm aware of that.

TOM: No one gets anything from me for nothing. I came from nothing. I'm climbing up there as fast as I can.

ADRIENNE: I understand.

TOM: People have taken more from me than they've ever given. Not any longer. T. Lomax is no longer here to be pushed around: he's learned his lesson. The fees are high where I come from. I call the tune. I'm the boss round here: if nobody likes it they know what to do.

[MRS DONALDSON *comes in from kitchen: takes dustpan and brush: glances at* TOM: *goes.*]

ADRIENNE: Does Carol sleep with other men?

TOM: What?

ADRIENNE: Does my sister sleep with men for money?

TOM: What do you think I am? A *pimp*?

ADRIENNE: I thought that's what you were. [*Direct, yet flinching.*]

TOM [*gazes at her for a moment*]: No one talks to me like that. No one. No man. No woman.

ADRIENNE: How would you describe yourself in that case, then?

TOM: I'm in business.

ADRIENNE: What business?

TOM: I sell pleasure. I hire pleasure out.

ADRIENNE: Do you hire my sister out?

TOM: . . . Your sister helps to run this place. Your sister is a businesswoman.

ADRIENNE: I have a little money, you see.

TOM: What?

ADRIENNE: Not much. A little. In addition to which I have the prospect of a great deal more.

TOM: You want to come in? You can pay for all the drink we had last night. Two of everything.

ADRIENNE: All right.

TOM: You agree.

ADRIENNE: If that's what you want. [*She watches him: he watches her.*]

TOM: You can pay for your lodging.

ADRIENNE: All right.

TOM: Were you at one time going to be famous?

ADRIENNE: I think so.

TOM: Like *I* might have been famous if I wasn't screwed up.

ADRIENNE: If you like.

TOM: Your husband was a bastard.

ADRIENNE: He was a very nice man.

TOM: My wife, too, was a very nice woman. *She* was a whore and I never knew it.

ADRIENNE: My husband was never like that.

TOM: This trip up here I can see has been no accident. What are you here for? To open up a provincial branch?

ADRIENNE: You could call it that.

[TOM *gazes at her: she gazes at him.*]

TOM: I'm onto your wavelength: you realize that.

ADRIENNE: I think we understand one another, if that's what you mean.

TOM [*gazes at her for a moment*]: This way of talking. You must teach me sometime. I'm not very good at talking: I was good at football. I could be a household word right now.

ADRIENNE: You speak very well. You make your feelings extremely clear. There are not many people who are able to do that.

[TOM *still gazes at her. Then:*]

ADRIENNE: You're very insecure.

TOM: Am I?

ADRIENNE: I think so. I wonder why it is.

TOM: I'm so insecure [*leaning over her*] I could put this in your face right now. [*Bunches fist before her.*]

ADRIENNE: You sound like Cracker.

TOM: That policeman does precisely what I tell him. I have friends in this town: no friend of mine has let me down. No *relation* of mine has let me down. This is a very self-sufficient business: everyone in this place pays their way.

[MRS DONALDSON *comes in from kitchen.*]

Will you clear out of this.

MRS DONALDSON: I'm tidying up.

TOM: This place is tidy enough already.

MRS DONALDSON: It hasn't been dusted.

TOM: Dust it tomorrow.

MRS DONALDSON: I shall, when I'm ready, dust it today.

[*Goes out to kitchen, having retrieved last of glasses, cups, etc., with backward look at* ADRIENNE.]

TOM: That trunk in the hall: nobody can get by it if it stays where it is.

ADRIENNE: I thought, initially, that was where you left it.

TOM: I left it there because I and the taxi-man could get it no further. Which is another one pound ten you owe me.

ADRIENNE: I'll ask the policeman to help when he comes again.

TOM: I am not carrying that trunk. I – this gentleman here – is not carrying that trunk anywhere.

ADRIENNE: In that case it will have to stay where it is.

TOM: If it's still there by twelve o'clock I'll get an axe and I'll chop it up. [*Still looking at her evenly.*]

ADRIENNE: I think, if I can find one, I'll have a drink. [*Goes to sideboard: looks: finds bottle, glass.*] Did you enjoy last night . . . ? [*Pours drink: looks at him.*]

TOM: I enjoyed it well enough.

ADRIENNE: Perhaps when you feel in the mood we can have another.

TOM: If you're paying for it.

ADRIENNE: That's right.

TOM: Same conditions: same enjoyment. I'll invite a few more of my clients round.

ADRIENNE: How many have you got?

TOM: A few.

ADRIENNE: Isn't it dangerous? [*Drinking.*] Can't you be prosecuted for a thing like that? [*Has crossed back to him.*]

TOM: They have to prove it first. Secondly, the sort of people who come here are a guarantee of immunity from this country's present hypocritical judicial system . . . Thirdly . . . thirdly: those two together make it impossible.

ADRIENNE: Don't the neighbours complain?

TOM: I give them free trips to the countryside. On top of which, one or two of them, if they can afford it, aren't above coming here themselves. Fourthly . . . [*She's still watching him.*] An arrangement like this isn't permanent.

ADRIENNE: Why not?

TOM: This isn't the only town on earth.

ADRIENNE: I wish I'd met you earlier.

TOM: That's right.

ADRIENNE: All the men I knew – in business – could never make their intentions clear. They floated with circumstances instead of trying to change them. [*Sits by him.*] My father was the opposite. He had lots of ideas – he was very attractive: he even had brains; but above all he had a surfeit of imagination – but without the practicality or the means to go with it.

TOM: I've heard about your father. I've heard about your spendthrift mother. No woman sells me out of *my* home: that from the beginning has been crystal clear. I use my brains: the people who come here are all my friends: we have a nice time: you'll know that. We had one such occasion here last night. In addition to which I'm a famous man: I was a prodigy: I was the youngest player at the time ever to play in First Division football. It lasted four years: then I got screwed up with my wife fornicating with another man.

ADRIENNE: My husband too has become a success. [*Flinching.*]

TOM: So I hear.

ADRIENNE: He's made a career in films.

TOM: He doesn't have anything to do with you.

ADRIENNE: He was ungrateful: he never acknowledged the things I did. *He* was unfaithful with another woman.

TOM: It goes on around you all the time.

ADRIENNE: How much would you want?

TOM: For what?

ADRIENNE [*flinching*]: To take half of what you earn.

TOM: I have three rooms in use in here: they're occupied most evenings of the week, and nearly all day on Saturday and Sunday. Sunday's an especially good day round here, particularly since the decline of organized religion. I have four girls in full-time occupation, and three part-timers who are married and have other things to do like running a home. Carol occasionally takes a job: she types: she was one man's private secretary for about a year: I nailed that bastard to his office chair. He'll never take a rise out of me again.

ADRIENNE: Carol is extremely loyal to you.

TOM: Like hell she is: she puts one foot out of line, she knows precisely where she stands.

[*Door from hall opens:* TERRY *comes in, fresh, pulling on jacket.*]

TERRY: Mrs Donaldson's gone off to phone. Have a nice day today. Can feel it.

TOM [*rising*]: I'm charging you for last night.

TERRY: I believe you said

TOM: And I'm charging her for all that coffee.

TERRY: Right.

TOM [*to* ADRIENNE]: I'll see you.

ADRIENNE: Right.

[TOM *gazes at her a moment: goes out through door to hall.*]

TERRY: How do you do it?

ADRIENNE: What?

TERRY: This transfiguration I noticed last night. It doesn't look normal.

ADRIENNE: I might ask the same of you: for instance – what are you doing in a place like this?

TERRY: I live here: at least, I half-live here.

ADRIENNE: I'd have thought a man your age, with your attraction, wouldn't need to resort to prostitutes.

TERRY: I never look at it like that. Everything here is so

informal. Despite Tom, it's always so friendly. I'm a respecter of women: I don't believe in their being abused. Are you really fond of Carol?

ADRIENNE: Yes.

TERRY: Do you really want her good?

ADRIENNE: That, I think, above everything.

TERRY: I wonder. [*Pause. Then:*] I'm sceptical, you see, about everything.

ADRIENNE: Do you have other girl-friends?

TERRY: Yes.

ADRIENNE: Do you always stick with Jo?

TERRY: I've been with Beryl. She's very tough. Jo's the one I'm fondest of. She's not the sort of girl I'd meet any other way. The girls I go around with formally are more like me . . . or Carol. She's restrained. She's probably like me in lots of ways: idealistic in a practical way. She married her prostitute: Tom is the whore who came up trumps.

[*Door bangs overhead.*

TERRY *looks up.*]

ADRIENNE [*stubbing out cigarette*]: I can see the attraction of a place like this.

TERRY: I like coming here. I can't afford it very often. When I get my next year's increment it'll be that bit easier. I might, even, become head of department, or have a post of responsibility. I could come here in that case almost every night. [*Laughs.*] When I'm headmaster I can take over the joint!

[*They laugh together:*

JOANNA *comes in from the hall. She's dressed in a short dressing-gown, her hair unbrushed.*]

JOANNA: There's a terrible row going on up there.

TERRY: Who with?

JOANNA: Carol. He's swearing at her something terrible. [*To* ADRIENNE] You're looking nice.

ADRIENNE: Thank you.

JOANNA: I didn't know you were down here as well.

TERRY: Day off school.

JOANNA: I suppose I shall have to ring up the office.

ADRIENNE: Do you work as well?

JOANNA: What would I do on my own at home? Everyone works around here. Everyone with *money*. It's not like paradise where you come from. What a night. I haven't enjoyed myself for ever so long.

[*Door slams violently overhead: she and* TERRY *look up.*] He'll kill her one day. I'm sure of that.

TERRY: What're they quarrelling about?

JOANNA: I've no idea.

TERRY: I better go up. [*To* ADRIENNE] Act as an intermediary.

JOANNA: Don't forget to duck.

TERRY: I shan't. [*Goes out through hall door.*]

JOANNA: Terry's convinced you're using drugs.

ADRIENNE: Is he?

JOANNA: It's to do with the shape of your eyes. [*Leans to her.*]

ADRIENNE: How much do you charge?

JOANNA: Enough.

ADRIENNE: Do you want to go on like this?

JOANNA: If I was happily married I don't think I would.

ADRIENNE: I don't see how your husband can be so compliant.

JOANNA: He doesn't like me very much. As opposed to which, he likes the money.

ADRIENNE: Why did you marry him?

JOANNA: I fell in love.

[ADRIENNE *leans forward suddenly for a cigarette.*]

130

In any case, I'll soon be too old. I might be divorced. I started here – not here exactly, but something like it – when I was only sixteen. My parents were separated and I lived in a home. [*Looks around.*] I think of this, in a way, as my home. I spend more time here than I do in my own. My husband doesn't work. He's saving up for something big. In the motor business: he'd like to start an accessories shop. I loved last night. It's the loveliest night we've had for years. Your dancing: it was ever so good.

    [*The door from the hall opens.*

    MRS DONALDSON *comes in: coat and woollen hat and gloves.*

    Adjoining room door slams violently.]

MRS DONALDSON: He's going to do something terrible: I can tell you that. [*To* JOANNA] Please go. Please go and talk to him, love.

JOANNA: I'll talk to her. I'll see what I can do. [*Goes out through hall door.*]

MRS DONALDSON: He's never been as violent as that. He can't stand to be crossed, I can tell you that . . .

    [*The door from the hall opens suddenly.*

    CAROL *comes in: wears simple dress and flat-heeled shoes.*

    JOANNA *enters with her.*]

Love! Are you all right?

CAROL: I'm fine. [*Looks round for somewhere to sit.*

    JOANNA *pulls out an upright chair.*]

JOANNA: Here. Here, love. Sit on that.

    [ADRIENNE *hasn't moved.*]

MRS DONALDSON: Let me get you something, love.

CAROL: I'll be all right. [*Wipes both eyes.*]

JOANNA: Here, then, love. Let's have a look.

CAROL: No, really. I'll be all right. I feel more dizzy than anything else.

[*Door slams violently off: silence.*]
I ought to go up and talk to him.
[*Pause.*]
JOANNA: Just leave him, love.
CAROL: He doesn't understand, you know. He's always been like this.
MRS DONALDSON: Just leave him, love. Terry's up there: he'll calm him down.
JOANNA: I should leave him altogether, love. He'll kill you one of these days. He doesn't know his own strength.
CAROL: He doesn't know any other way, you see. [*Aware suddenly of* ADRIENNE.] Last night was so lovely, Aid. It really was. [*To* MRS DONALDSON] He hates to be criticized. He can't stand criticism from anyone.
ADRIENNE: Can I get you anything, Carol?
CAROL: No, love. I'm sorry that you've had to see it. [*Wipes her eye.*] I think I'm going to be sick. [*Gets up quickly and goes out to the kitchen, followed by* JOANNA.
ADRIENNE, *after a moment, gets another cigarette having stubbed out the other.*]
ADRIENNE: Do you smoke, Mrs Donaldson?
MRS DONALDSON: No thanks.
[ADRIENNE *lights it.*]
MRS DONALDSON: If people aren't friendly I don't know where I am. [*Distracted.*] I can't stand hate. I can't stand people to hate one another.
ADRIENNE: I'm sure it'll pass.
MRS DONALDSON: I'll make some tea. Do you want some, love?
ADRIENNE: No thanks.
[MRS DONALDSON *goes out to kitchen.*
ADRIENNE *looks round her. Goes to sideboard: about to pour another drink:*
TERRY *comes in from hall.*]

TERRY: I'll have one of those. [*Holds out hands.*] Can't keep still. Just look. [*Takes the drink* ADRIENNE *pours: swallows it.*] He ought to be certified. Or is the spontaneous expression of feeling a sign of health? I'll have to think that over. Is to come out with what you feel the truer road to progress? [*Drinks again.*] Where's Carol?

ADRIENNE: In the kitchen.

TERRY: Tom's gone off. He'll be back again quite shortly. He won't leave this house unguarded for long.

ADRIENNE: Why is he so absorbed by the house?

TERRY: It's the only thing he's got. All that he's left from his famous busted marriage. It's not even his; it's owned by the council and he has to pay rent. There's some scheme, however, whereby council tenants, after a certain number of years, will become eligible to buy the freehold of their homes. [*Finishes drink: gasps.*] My cerebral life doesn't prepare me for events like this: it doesn't prepare me as a matter of fact for anything at all.

ADRIENNE: Except talking about lakes.

TERRY: Lakes and streams and rivers and glaciers. [*Pause: glances at her.*] I could never beat up a woman, however strongly I felt: however badly she'd done to me. It's his first wife he's beating when he starts to hit Carol. He lived in a man's world that came apart: whoring, screwing and fighting, with his wife and children safely back home. But the wife back home didn't have any children, and she didn't sit down in the face of his whoring, and she refused to idolize him when he became a star, and she went off in the end like he did and screwed someone else, and Tom, with his simple view of the world, that men should be men and that women should submit, found that the parts wouldn't fit together. This holds the remnants [*Gestures round.*] this and Carol who loves him I suppose for the desperate man he is. A brothel keeper has become his true vocation, his vision of a world where women are screwed and men enjoy themselves. It's only because of Carol that it's something else: she takes the bitterness out of it and makes it – something real, I guess.

[*The door from the kitchen opens.*

MRS DONALDSON *comes in with tray: teapot, cups, jug and sugar. She's still dressed in her outdoor hat, minus coat and gloves.*]

Did you get down and phone the school?

MRS DONALDSON: The school will be able to manage without you for a little longer. [*To* ADRIENNE] When I got back I *heard* the shouting: I went up to talk to them. [*To* TERRY] I think he was beginning to hit her then. [*To* ADRIENNE] Did you know your sister was pregnant?

ADRIENNE: No.

MRS DONALDSON: She's four months. Nearly five.

TERRY: Good God.

MRS DONALDSON: This is the sort of life a child comes into!

[*Door from the kitchen opens.*

CAROL *comes in with* JOANNA.]

TERRY: Are you all right?

CAROL: I think so.

TERRY [*to* JOANNA]: The one place he always goes for: eyes. Have you noticed that? There must be some psychological explanation of that.

CAROL: Has he gone out?

TERRY: He went for a walk. He'll be back in a jiffy. [*To* ADRIENNE] His rages, you see, don't last very long.

CAROL: He won't be back. He'll have gone to Beryl's.

ADRIENNE: Why Beryl's?

CAROL: That's where he goes. He sends her husband out. [*To* TERRY] He doesn't like doing it here. It's what we quarrelled about this morning: he wanted Beryl to stay the night. In the end, when I talked to her, she went back

134

home. He'll have gone there now. He couldn't forgive me. He hates to be disparaged. He hates to be found out. I don't understand. [*Blows her nose: wipes her eyes finally.*] Why do men need to sleep with so many women? Why isn't it sacred to one woman or not at all?

TERRY: Some hostess, love, to be asking that.

CAROL: I am asking. I'd like to know.

TERRY: Ask Jo. She knows more about it than any of us.

JOANNA: I've never thought it's that important. Isn't it to do with when sex was a secret?

CAROL: No. It's not.

JOANNA: Then I don't know what it's to do with, love.

MRS DONALDSON [*handing* CAROL *a cup of tea she's poured*]: Are you all right, love?

CAROL: I think so.

MRS DONALDSON: Jo: would you like a cup?

JOANNA: No thanks.

MRS DONALDSON: Adrienne?

    [ADRIENNE *shakes her head.*
    She glances at TERRY: *he shakes his head.*]

I'll just go out and clear the kitchen. [*Goes.*]

JOANNA: I'll have to be going soon as well. *Some* row I'll have when *I* get in.

CAROL: Stay here if you like, love.

JOANNA: I better get back. As soon as I know you're feeling all right.

CAROL: Oh, I'm all right. More'll be here. And Adrienne.

JOANNA: I shouldn't let him back into the house if I were you. Not until he's apologized, or made a promise. [*To* ADRIENNE] You could bolt the doors and windows.

CAROL: He'd break the glass. It's his house. Deprive him of that and I think he'd go mad. [*To* ADRIENNE] He was once such a wonderful footballer. Three years ago there was a film on television about some player of today, showing how he was seven years ago, and during the film there was a shot of Tom – he must have been nineteen at the time – and in the middle of this move he took the ball – it was beautiful: he beat four men in front of goal, then passed to this older man who scored. It was really . . . I don't know what it was. [*To* TERRY] There are no words to describe it . . . Someone who can really win.

TERRY: If I went now I could get in by lunch: do the afternoon and the Head wouldn't feel so bad.

CAROL: You go, love. Don't let this jeopardize your career.

TERRY: Oh, this is my career: the rest is just indulgence, love. [*Stoops to* CAROL: *kisses her cheek.*] I'll see you, then. Bye, Jo.

JOANNA: Goodbye.

TERRY: You'll be here next time, I suppose.

ADRIENNE: That's right.

[TERRY *goes out through hall door.*]

TERRY [*heard, calling*]: Bye, Mrs D.

MRS DONALDSON [*heard*]: All right.

[*Outside front door slams.*
Pause.]

CAROL: He gave Terry a terrible beating. I don't think anyone can contain him when he gets like that. I've never seen him as angry as that. It's all frustration: it's all energy he's not sure how to use.

JOANNA: If you don't want me, love, I'll go up and get dressed.

CAROL: Right.

[JOANNA *nods at* ADRIENNE: *goes out by hall door.*
Pause.]

ADRIENNE: Do you want some more tea?

CAROL: No thanks.

ADRIENNE: Mrs Donaldson said you were pregnant.

CAROL: Yes.

ADRIENNE: Nearly five months.

CAROL: Yes.

ADRIENNE: Do you feel all right?

CAROL: I think so.

ADRIENNE: I had a child.

CAROL: He told me, love.

ADRIENNE: I wouldn't like to see that happen again.

CAROL: It won't. [*Suddenly*] I'm tougher than you. I look after myself. I don't live in fantasies. I live here on earth.

ADRIENNE: I'll have another drink.

CAROL: Do you have to? It's there for entertaining, love, not for swilling down like food.

ADRIENNE: In that case I won't.

CAROL: Tom says you even made him an offer.

ADRIENNE: I have some money.

CAROL: To set up a *brothel*?

ADRIENNE: It's what you work in.

CAROL: I live with Tom. I'm trying to change him. I'm trying to drag him out of this mess. I want to salvage something from it.

ADRIENNE: He doesn't want to change.

CAROL: No one wants to change, my love. *You* have to change: and by you changing they change also. You have to educate them, Aid. He was brought up in a world of opportunists, of grabbing what you can, by measuring your life by what you've achieved. I want him to change: I want him to be able to lose all that. You talking to him like that isn't going to help me much.

ADRIENNE: I thought I was trying to help. I was trying to reassure him.

CAROL: You're like our father. Father would dress up like the King of the Town: he would talk for hours, plausibly, about the most improbable schemes. He had a tongue and charm like you: he had the same gullibility and energy, the same sense of occasion, the same vulnerability, the same capacity for defeat. He too could talk the leg off a donkey: he'd convince anyone of anything for the time it took to swallow a drink: when the bills came in the plausibility had gone. It was some other scheme. This man you married.

ADRIENNE: What?

CAROL: I've been reading these cuttings. You weren't married to this star – this now so famous star – at all.

ADRIENNE: You've been talking to someone behind my back.

CAROL: It says in this famous cutting this man never married.

ADRIENNE: It's lying. It has it all wrong. I was married. I have been married.

CAROL: Who to?

ADRIENNE: To someone.

CAROL: Who? Who for God's sake, love? Get these fantasies out of your mind!

ADRIENNE: I was married! He wasn't any good. He left me finally. He lives with a woman. I still am married, Carol. He never divorced me.

CAROL: Aid. What're you trying to do to yourself?

ADRIENNE: I loved him. I still love him. I love him, Carol, like you love Tom. [Weeps.]

CAROL: Aid, for God's sake. [Comes to her.] I'm not getting at you. I want to help you. [Holds her.]

ADRIENNE: I've run away.

CAROL: You've run away from what?

ADRIENNE: From a place.

CAROL: What sort of place?

ADRIENNE: From a home.

CAROL: What home?

[ADRIENNE *shakes her head, her face hidden.*]

CAROL: What home?

ADRIENNE: He put me there. I told him he would. A man shouldn't do that to a woman. I can't stand betrayal: I can't stand it. I can't stand a man saying he loves you and all the time he's saying it he's making love to another woman.

CAROL: What is it, Aid?

ADRIENNE: I can't stand people not loving me! I can't stand it, Carol. I can't stand it. I can't stand people betraying my love!

CAROL: Look, now, love. You're safe. You're here. [*Embraces her.*] We're both together. We're sisters. We love one another, you see, so much.

ADRIENNE: He came to my room.

CAROL: Who?

ADRIENNE: Last night. He came to my room. I'm sure I was drunk. I felt so happy. I have pills to take. I shouldn't drink on top of them. I thought it was Terry.

CAROL: What?

ADRIENNE: I can't bear it, love.

CAROL: Aid.

ADRIENNE: It's why he's so angry.

CAROL: Aid.

ADRIENNE: I felt so happy. I felt so complete.

CAROL: *Who* came to your room?

ADRIENNE: Tom. [*Grasps her more firmly.*] I wanted to enjoy the evening so much! I wanted it to be so marvellous. I did so want to feel alive! I wanted to be someone that everyone admired.

CAROL: Aid . . . You're making this up.

ADRIENNE: I wanted to help you. I can help you. Believe me. I don't want to go back. I can't describe what it's like to you, Carol. I could have done so many things. I had a child . . . he didn't believe in me at all. He didn't believe in me one bit. I told him I could change the world. I tried. I tried. I really tried to change it, love.

[CAROL *releases her.*]

I had an accident. I took too many pills. I hadn't meant to do anything like that at all. He told the police. I went to hospital. It was like a dream. After he left I couldn't wake up. I tried. I tried. The doctor ordered me to stay inside. I begged. I pleaded. I got down on my knees. I had a friend, an actress; she came to see me twice. Then she got a job out of town and couldn't come: she wrote. After that there was no one else. He never came to see me again. There was no one I could turn to, love. You can't imagine what it's like in there: the people, Carol. It's worse than hell: it's all fastened up, you see, inside. I had a trunk. I wrote you a letter. I said I'd come and see you. I got out at night, just before the ward was closed. No one will know I'm even here: no one will look: no one cares about me at all. I *can* become something. I know it inside. I know that, Carol, as sure as I know anything at all.

CAROL: I shall have to find Tom.

ADRIENNE: I shall never, never, never, on my heart, Carol, never do a thing like that again.

CAROL [*calls*]: Mrs Donaldson!

ADRIENNE: Don't waste your life on him. He'll only bring you what I've had, love.

[MRS DONALDSON *comes in: apron on as in Act One: no hat. Enters from kitchen.*]

CAROL: Would you sit with my sister. You might get her some coffee. But nothing to drink.

MRS DONALDSON: All right, then, love.

CAROL: I'm looking for Tom. I shan't be long. [*Goes. Pause.*]

MRS DONALDSON: Would you like some coffee?

ADRIENNE: No thanks.

MRS DONALDSON: I haven't recovered, you know, from last night.

ADRIENNE: No.

MRS DONALDSON: At least this is looking a bit more tidy.

ADRIENNE: Yes. [*Pause.*] You don't have to sit here. I feel quite well enough. It was only a momentary indisposition. I'm feeling fine.

MRS DONALDSON: All right, then, love. I'll be in the kitchen if you want me.

ADRIENNE: Right.

> [MRS DONALDSON *takes tray of tea things, and* CAROL's *cup, and goes out to kitchen.*
> ADRIENNE *pauses: goes to sideboard: hesitates over drink: brushes back her hair.*
> *Door from hall opens.*
> JOANNA *enters: thick coat, scarf, gloves.*]

JOANNA: Is Carol out?

ADRIENNE: Yes.

JOANNA: Where's she gone?

ADRIENNE: She's looking for her husband.

JOANNA: A glutton for punishment, I'll tell you that. [*Pulls on gloves.*] I'll see you, love.

ADRIENNE: Right.

JOANNA: Bye.

ADRIENNE: Goodbye.

> [JOANNA *goes.*
> ADRIENNE *looks round her: goes to curtains: absent-mindedly rearranges them: doesn't look out. Turns back to room: holds head.*
> *Sound of outside door closing.*
> *She waits.*
> *Door from hall finally opens.*

141

CRAWFORD *enters in uniform, cap in hand: genial, relaxed.*]

CRAWFORD: You here.

ADRIENNE: Yes.

CRAWFORD: On your own?

ADRIENNE: Yes.

CRAWFORD: I've just seen Jo. At the gate outside.

ADRIENNE: Yes.

CRAWFORD: Mrs Donaldson in the kitchen: gets through some cleaning. I can tell you that.

ADRIENNE: Yes.

CRAWFORD: I just dropped by. Say thanks for last night.

ADRIENNE: Would you like a drink?

CRAWFORD: Make it a vodka. Can't smell it on the breath. [*Puts down cap on table.*] On duty.

ADRIENNE: Right.

CRAWFORD: You enjoy it?

ADRIENNE: Yes.

CRAWFORD: Not often have evenings like that.

ADRIENNE: No?

CRAWFORD [*takes drink: downs it neat*]: Best way. Like life. Short and sweet. My philosophy. Likely to be back, then, is she?

ADRIENNE: I don't know. [*Brushes back her hair.*]

CRAWFORD: Looking smart.

ADRIENNE: Thank you.

CRAWFORD: You've preserved your figure very well.

ADRIENNE: I've tried to take care of it. In my work it becomes essential.

[CRAWFORD *embraces her.*]

Please don't.

CRAWFORD: There's nobody here.

ADRIENNE: Please don't.

CRAWFORD: Fit in here, you know. Don't stand on ceremony. No malingerers here, tha knows.

ADRIENNE: Please don't.

CRAWFORD: Come next door. Reserved for special occasions is that. Special occasions: I've only used it once myself.

ADRIENNE: Please leave me alone.

CRAWFORD: I arrest you, you know, in the name of the law! [*Takes her, his arm strongly round her waist, to the hall door.*] Be in and out inside a minute.

ADRIENNE: Please leave me!

CRAWFORD: It'll be over in a minute. No need to take any time at all.

ADRIENNE: No!

> [*Door from the kitchen opens:*
> MRS DONALDSON *comes in.*]

MRS DONALDSON: There's a car outside.

CRAWFORD: Is there?

MRS DONALDSON: Yours then, is it.

CRAWFORD: Mine, Mrs Donaldson, is around the corner. I don't leave it parked outside this house. I have learnt one or two tricks of the trade, tha knows.

MRS DONALDSON [*at window*]: Been up once and come back again. [*Turns to* CRAWFORD.] Looking at the numbers. [*Turns back to window.*] Gone off the other end. Looking at the odds and evens.

CRAWFORD: Expecting anybody, are you?

MRS DONALDSON: No.

CRAWFORD: If that's the case, then we'll be all right.

MRS DONALDSON: Right.

> [MRS DONALDSON *glances inquiringly at* ADRIENNE: *goes back out to kitchen.*
> ADRIENNE *stands there.*
> *Outer door bangs:*]

CAROL [*heard*]: More!

MRS DONALDSON [*heard*]: Yes, love?

CAROL [*heard*]: Has Tom come back?

MRS DONALDSON [*heard*]: No, love.

CAROL [*heard*]: I want you a minute.

[*Sound of door closing, off.*

Silence.

Pause.]

CRAWFORD [*picks up cap*]: Best get back, then. [*Pause: looks at her.*] Staying long, then, are you?

ADRIENNE: I may be staying for quite some time. I may be going into business.

CRAWFORD: What sort of business?

ADRIENNE: I have one or two . . . propositions I need to look into. I have a little capital to invest and one or two suggestions have already been made. One is being considered at the moment.

CRAWFORD [*gazes at her*]: Likely, then, I'll see you.

ADRIENNE: I'll be around, I think, for quite some time.

CRAWFORD: Right. I'll look forward to that. [*Confidentially*] The material round here isn't all to my liking as a matter of fact. A change of ingredients wouldn't go astray. As for the management: one or two improvements theer would go a very long way in my book.

[*Door slams off.*]

I'll see you, then.

[CAROL *comes in from hall: dressed as before, without an outside coat.*]

CAROL: You leaving, then?

CRAWFORD: Just popped in to say hello.

CAROL: Hello.

CRAWFORD: Give due thanks for the party, tha knows.

CAROL: Thanks.

CRAWFORD: Goodbye.

CAROL: Goodbye.

[CRAWFORD *glances across at* ADRIENNE: *goes, leaving by hall door.*

Pause.
Outer door closes.]

ADRIENNE: I was going to get dressed.

CAROL: Yes.

ADRIENNE: Into something a little more decent. I look such a sight.

CAROL: It looks all right to me.

ADRIENNE: Did you see your husband?

CAROL: No.

ADRIENNE: Perhaps he's gone to Beryl's.

CAROL: I doubt it now.

ADRIENNE [*flinches*]: Oh.

CAROL: He'll be walking round. Waiting for me, in fact, to find him.

ADRIENNE: Is that what he does?

CAROL: He's like a child. I have to consider him as a man, however.

ADRIENNE: Carol, you know, I need you so much.

CAROL: Yes.

ADRIENNE: I have no one else. There are things that I do that I can never help. I have all sorts of plans. I could even help *you*. I've got some capital put by: I was telling Tom. Why are you looking at me? Is something wrong?

CAROL: No.

ADRIENNE: Is it my hair?

CAROL: It looks perfectly all right.

ADRIENNE: Crawford made advances to me. Men fall in love with me. It's been like that for as long as I remember. There's nothing I can do. Wherever I go they are all the same. I'm so *conditioned*. The doctor told me. But if I'm not a woman what can I be? Men only want one thing: love and tenderness is the way they get it, then after that they go away. We could live together. We could both live together in a house again. It would be like we were: we could share the same room. We could see where things went wrong and put them right. We could bring up your child: *our* child: it could be the one I lost. You see: things are never as black as they first appear.

CAROL: There's a car outside.

ADRIENNE: Mrs Donaldson said there was a car. She mentioned it to Crawford: she thought it was his.

CAROL: The woman who is in it is waiting outside. Someone who's come a long way to see you.

ADRIENNE: Who?

CAROL: She wants you to leave with her, Aid.

ADRIENNE: I haven't packed. I haven't done anything at all this morning.

CAROL: Mrs Donaldson is packing already.

ADRIENNE: I sent no forwarding address or anything.

CAROL: They had an address. Your next of kin.

ADRIENNE: Of course. [*Gazes at her in horror.*] I must have forgot. All I had left, you see, was you. [*Gazes at her.*] I don't think I can bear to leave. I have nowhere else to go.

CAROL: This is no place. Unless you have somewhere else to go they're obliged to take you back.

ADRIENNE: I *could* stay here. I promise to behave. I have my pills. You can supervise them. I can help with the baby: I can help with all manner of things.

[*Door from the hall opens.*

TOM *enters: jacket open, collar of shirt open, tieless: has just come in: looks from* CAROL *to* ADRIENNE *and back again.*]

CAROL: There's no one could really look after you here. These people, these medical people, what would they think? This is no place for you to get better.

ADRIENNE: I can take care of myself. There's nothing wrong with me. I promise. [*Looks desperately at* TOM. *Then at* CAROL]: Carol: you're all I have on earth.

146

CAROL: I can't take care of you, Aid. I have more than enough as it is, already.

ADRIENNE: I want you!

CAROL: I can't.

ADRIENNE: I *need* you! Please, believe me! These people: you've no idea what it's like in there. This money: you can have it. I don't want it. You can have my clothes. Please. Carol. Don't let me go.

CAROL: You'll have to go. For your own sake, Aid. I have no choice.

ADRIENNE: If I go in there I'll never come out.

CAROL: You will come out.

ADRIENNE: I won't. I'll be in there, Carol, for the rest of my life. I'll become a whore: perhaps when I'm a whore you'll want me back.

CAROL: You'll have to go. I have no choice. Out of all this mess I have to extricate something, Aid.

ADRIENNE: *He'll* extricate it for you: he'll tear that child clean out of you! I had my child torn out: I had my creation wrenched out by a man! I had my child torn out alive. In *me*. For ever. It was never *born*!

[TOM *goes to door to the hall.*]

Don't let that woman in here! I want no one else in here at all!

[TOM *pauses.*

They wait.]

I'm always nervous at a time like this. When something really big comes up. You wait for it, Carol, all your life. Then, when it comes . . . I act like this. *Don't touch me!*

[TOM *has made a slight move towards her. They wait, the door of the room open.*]

Families are an illusion, Carol. You have to destroy them to stay alive. [*Makes move to door: pauses.*

CAROL *makes move to her.*]

I'll go alone. [*Pauses: tenses: goes.*

147

Pause.
Then:
Heard: screams]: *No!*
[*Front door closes off.*
They wait.
Pause.
TOM *moves to window.*]

CAROL: Has she gone?
[TOM *watches at the window a moment, curtain up: then, after a moment:*]

TOM: They've taken her off.
[*Sound of car fades.*
TOM *turns to room: goes to sideboard: pours drink: holds up glass, offering.*
CAROL *hasn't moved: hand on her stomach.*
TOM *shrugs. Then:*]
Well. [*Drinks: toasts.*] Back to reality again, I reckon.
[*Light fades.*]

LIFE CLASS

This play was first presented at the Royal Court Theatre, London, on 9 April 1974, under the direction of Lindsay Anderson. The cast was as follows:

ALLOTT	Alan Bates
WARREN	Stephen Bent
SAUNDERS	Frank Grimes
STELLA	Rosemary Martin
MATHEWS	Paul Kelly
BRENDA	Sally Watts
CARTER	David Lincoln
CATHERINE	Gabrielle Lloyd
MOONEY	Stewart Rayner
GILLIAN	Brenda Cavendish
ABERCROMBIE	Bob Peck
FOLEY	Brian Glover
PHILIPS	Gerald James

CHARACTERS

ALLOTT

WARREN

SAUNDERS

STELLA

MATHEWS

BRENDA

CARTER

CATHERINE

MOONEY

GILLIAN

ABERCROMBIE

FOLEY

PHILIPS

ACT ONE

A stage.

Off-centre, stage right, is a wooden platform, some six to eight feet square, on castors.

Beside it are two metal stands, about six feet high, each equipped with two vertical flat-plane heaters. Scattered around the platform are two or three easels and several wooden 'donkeys': low, rectangular stools with an upright T-shaped bar at one end. On one, folded, is a white sheet. There are two brown hessian screens, one upstage centre, the other centre left. Upstage left is a rack with coatpegs. ALLOTT *comes in stage left. In his late thirties, medium-build, he wears a duffle-coat, battered trilby hat and gloves. Blows in his hands. Thumps gloves. Shivers. Looks round. Goes over to the wall, switches on the heaters, comes back, takes off gloves, feels plates. Warms one hand, then the other: looks round, puts gloves back on. Steps back. Examines platform, head on one side. Contemplates. Returns to platform: pushes it into new position: contemplates: adjusts it slightly.*

WARREN *comes in: young, well-built: overcoat and scarf. Stays at one side.*

WARREN: Morning, sir.
ALLOTT: Morning, Warren.
　　　[WARREN *watches* ALLOTT *a while adjusting platform.*]
WARREN: . . . Nobody else here then, yet, Mr Allott.
ALLOTT [*pays* WARREN *no attention*]: Perfectly correct.
WARREN: Er . . . cold.
ALLOTT: Very.
WARREN: Get a cup of tea.
ALLOTT: That's right.

WARREN: Well . . . See you.

ALLOTT: Hope so.

WARREN: Yeh. [*Last look round: he goes.*

    ALLOTT *steps back: contemplates. Goes over to heater: carries it round to the platform's new position.*

    SAUNDERS *comes in: thin, anaemic; raincoat, young.*]

SAUNDERS: Morning, sir.

ALLOTT: Saunders.

SAUNDERS: Need any help, sir?

ALLOTT: Let's see. [*Takes off gloves: takes off coat.*] Could hang that up somewhere. [*Then hat.*] And that.

SAUNDERS: Right. [*Takes them.*]

ALLOTT: Er. . . . Over there, I think . . . That's right . . . Now, then. Chalk. Pencil. [*Feels in jacket pockets: checks.*] Toilet paper . . . Seen Mr Philips, have you?

SAUNDERS: No, sir.

ALLOTT: Had some unfinished business there, I recollect.

SAUNDERS: Anything else, sir?

ALLOTT: No . . . Yes. Could chalk the platform. There's a lad. [*Hands him chalk.*]

SAUNDERS: Right.

ALLOTT: Shan't be a sec . . . [*Hesitates. Looks round.*] . . . Right. [*He goes.*

    SAUNDERS *chalks off the corners of the platform on the floor.*

    As he reaches the third corner, STELLA *comes in: a model, in her twenties: she's muffled up in a heavy coat and cap: carries a shopping-bag as well as a handbag.*]

STELLA: Freezing. [*Shivers: goes directly to the heater.*]

SAUNDERS: Just setting this . . .

STELLA: Mr Allott here?

SAUNDERS: He's just gone out . . .

STELLA: You wouldn't pop these in the cubicle, would you, love?

SAUNDERS: Yes. [*Takes the bag and handbag.*]

STELLA: Do my shopping on the way up. Get in early . . .
Worth all the trouble . . . I'll be in the . . . Shan't be long.
[*She goes.*
SAUNDERS *crosses to the upstage screen: takes bags behind.*
Pause.
MATHEWS *comes in: he's followed by* BRENDA.
MATHEWS *wears a windcheater. He's smoking.* BRENDA
wears a coat: both are young.
MATHEWS *drops his cigarette, treads it out.*]

MATHEWS: Brenda: have a ride . . .

BRENDA: Not likely . . . Been on there before.
[MATHEWS *pushes the platform like a trolley: jumps on for*
a ride: screams out.]

MATHEWS: Smashing . . .

SAUNDERS [*coming back*]: Here . . . I'm just marking that.
[*He takes the platform from* MATHEWS *and pushes it back.*]

BRENDA [*to* SAUNDERS]: Allott here, then, is he?

SAUNDERS: Yeh.

MATHEWS: Gone down to the bog. I bet he has . . . Spends
bloody hours in there, he does.

BRENDA: Not the only one, I think.

MATHEWS: Writes bloody poetry . . . Ask Warren . . .
Saunders: isn't that right?

SAUNDERS: You've made a mess of this . . . I can't find the
other mark.

MATHEWS: Come on. Come on. Over here . . . that's right.
[*Helps him.*]

BRENDA: So cold . . . [*Shivers, standing by the heater.*] Shan't
do anything today . . . Just look . . . Can hardly hold a
pencil. Dropping off. [*Holds up her hands.*]

MATHEWS: Ought to walk here.

BRENDA: Walk here?

LIFE CLASS

MATHEWS: Do you good . . . I walk every morning, as a matter of fact.
BRENDA: I've seen you.
MATHEWS: Eyes'll drop out one day.
BRENDA: Tell her you're an artist, do you?
MATHEWS: Don't need to tell her . . . Can tell it at a glance.
BRENDA: Here. Saunders. Should have seen him. Mathews – walking: hand in hand.
MATHEWS: What's the matter with hand in hand?
BRENDA: Your grubby hands . . . You want to wash them.
MATHEWS: A damn sight cleaner, love, than yours. [*Grapples with her: takes her.*]
BRENDA: Get off! . . . Go on! . . . *Get off!*
CARTER [*entering*]: Here. Here. Here. What's going on in here?
[CARTER *is small, stocky, genial: dressed in jeans and a zip-jacket, young.*]
MATHEWS: She's molesting me, Kenneth . . . Ever since I came in . . . Follows me around. Just look.
[*Having been released by* MATHEWS *at* CARTER'S *entrance,* BRENDA *has followed him around to hit him back: now, however, she moves off.*]
CARTER: Allott here, then, is he?
MATHEWS: In the bog.
CARTER: Ay . . . is it true, then? Sits in there . . . who told me?
MATHEWS: Warren . . .
CARTER: Writing verses in a book.
[MATHEWS *laughs.*]
BRENDA: What's the matter with writing that?
MATHEWS: Shan't say a word . . . [*Moves off. Then:*] Should read some of it, my love.
BRENDA: Better than the stuff you write . . . Did you hear that Foley caught him writing on the stairs?

156

CARTER: Here . . .

BRENDA: On the wall.

SAUNDERS: What was that, then, Mathews?

CARTER: Go on, then. What did he say?

MATHEWS: Nothing . . .

CARTER: Come on. Come on, then. [*To* BRENDA] What did he write?

BRENDA: Dunno . . . Had to wash it off.

MATHEWS: Bloody obsessionalist, that man . . . Should see a doctor.

CARTER: Come on . . . Come on . . . When was it?

BRENDA: Aren't you going to tell us, Bryan?

MATHEWS: Tell you bloody nothing . . . Mouth like a gramophone. Yak, yak, yak . . .

BRENDA: 'Mr Foley is feeling poorly': that's the sort of stuff he used to write.

CARTER: Brenda: how about it, love? [*Embraces her: sway together.*]

SAUNDERS: I've marked that platform: nobody move it.

CARTER: Shan't touch it. No. We shan't. We shan't. [*Hums to himself: sways with* BRENDA.

    MATHEWS *picks spots on his face, standing resentfully to one side.*]

BRENDA [*sings*]: Have you ever . . .
                Asked me whether . . .

CARTER [*sings*]: No, I've never . . .
                Asked you whether.

BRENDA [*sings*]: I would ever . . .

CARTER [*sings*]: You would ever . . . .

BRENDA [*sings*]: Dance the whole night long with you!
    [*They laugh, embracing.*

CATHERINE *comes in: late teens: dressed in a long coat and cap; carries a large straw bag. Panting, sets down her bag by a donkey: takes off cap.*]

4

CATHERINE: Run up all those stairs . . . Do it every morning. Exercise, you know.

MATHEWS: Could run up somewhere else with me, love. [*Guffaws.*

CATHERINE *glances over: otherwise disregarding: takes off gloves.*

BRENDA *has disengaged herself from* CARTER: *she crosses over to* CATHERINE.]

BRENDA: Did you bring it with you?

CATHERINE: Here, then: have a look.

[*She gets a hat from the straw bag: tries it on for* BRENDA's *approval.*

MATHEWS *crosses over to* CARTER.]

CARTER: Got a fag?

MATHEWS: Last one.

CARTER: Sammy?

SAUNDERS: Got a pipe.

MATHEWS: Joking.

SAUNDERS: No, then . . . [*Gets one out: puts it in his mouth.*]

MATHEWS: Here . . . [*Takes it: tries it in his own mouth.*] How d'I look?

CARTER [*ignoring* MATHEWS]: How long have you had a pipe, then, Sammy?

SAUNDERS: A week or two . . . Smoke it in the evenings.

CARTER: Evenings.

SAUNDERS: Just before I go to bed.

MATHEWS: Do summat else, personally, just afore I go to bed. [*Laughs, pipe between his teeth.*

CARTER *takes the pipe from him and gives it back to* SAUNDERS.

WARREN *comes in, dressed as before.*]

WARREN: Somebody's got here, then, have they? Be half of 'em away today.

CARTER: Seen Allott, have you?

WARREN: Yeh. Came in before . . . Morning, Brenda . . . Morning, Catherine.

BRENDA *and* CATHERINE [*together*]: Morning, Warren.

WARREN: Nice day for it. What d'you think?

BRENDA: Lovely.

WARREN: That your hat, then?

[BRENDA *has now tried it.*]

BRENDA: Catherine's.

CATHERINE: Do you like it?

WARREN: Dunno . . . [CATHERINE *tries it.*] Suits her. [*Indicating* CATHERINE.]

BRENDA: Thank you. Just what I was hoping.

MATHEWS: Here . . . give us a try, then, love. [*Snatches it from her head.*]

CATHERINE: Come here . . . Give it back . . . It cost a lot of money did that hat . . . [*Walks after him as* MATHEWS *dances away, the hat on his head.*]

MATHEWS: Here . . . here . . . How d'I look?

BRENDA: Give it back . . .

MATHEWS: Come and get it . . . Sammy: how d'I look? [*Dances on to the platform.*]

ALLOTT [*entering*]: You the new model, are you, Mathews . . . ? Bit over to the right. Lovely . . . Lower your trousers and I think we'll be all right.

[*They all laugh:* MATHEWS *gets down moodily from the platform.*

CATHERINE *takes her hat.*]

Spend more time getting ready for what you have to do . . . turning your thoughts to higher things . . . time and space . . . the eternal verities . . . wouldn't do you any harm. Your hat, is it, Catherine?

CATHERINE: Yes, sir.

ALLOTT: Very nice . . . [*To* SAUNDERS] Stella arrived, then, has she?

SAUNDERS: Yes, sir . . . Said she wouldn't be long.

CARTER: Composed any poems this morning, sir?

ALLOTT: What?

MATHEWS: Poems, sir.

> [*The girls giggle.*
> ALLOTT *pauses. Then:*]

ALLOTT: If we could have a little application . . . tools of the trade . . . Catherine: I should put away your hat.

> [DEREK MOONEY *and* GILLIAN STAFFORD *come in.* MOONEY *has long hair.* GILLIAN *is slender.*]

MOONEY: Are we late, sir?

ALLOTT: No, no, Mooney. Just in time . . . Gillian.

GILLIAN: Morning, sir.

ALLOTT: Looks to me as if half our members are going to be away today . . . Colds. 'Flu . . . Distemper . . . Myxomatosis . . . What do you think, Carter?

CARTER: Yes, sir. Weather like this.

ALLOTT: Seen anyone on your travels, Mooney?

MOONEY: No, sir.

ALLOTT: Except Gillian, of course.

MOONEY: Yes, sir.

ALLOTT: One day I'll find one of you two alone.

WARREN: What will you do then, sir?

ALLOTT: I shall tell – the him or her as the case may be – certain relevant facts, Warren.

WARREN: What about, sir?

ALLOTT: Facts which may well lead – the him or her as the case may be – to revise their opinion about the other . . . him or her, as the case may be.

CARTER: Tell us now, sir.

BRENDA: What secrets have you got, sir?

ALLOTT: Sammy: everything in order, is it?

SAUNDERS: Yes, sir.

MOONEY: What facts are they, sir?

CATHERINE: Gillian's dying to know, sir!

ALLOTT: It's you, Mooney, I'm worried about . . . Has it ever struck you, for instance, that you've another fifty or sixty years to live?

MOONEY: Yes, sir.

ALLOTT: How about you, Gillian?

GILLIAN: Yes, sir.

ALLOTT: Doesn't that come as a terrible shock?

GILLIAN: No, sir.

ALLOTT: You'll be tired of this long-haired ninny by the time short hair comes in again.

MOONEY: I'll get it cut.

ALLOTT: She won't love you with it cut. Will you, Jilly?

GILLIAN: I don't know . . . I like it long.

MOONEY: Here, sir . . .!

ALLOTT: Sammy: how about these stools?

SAUNDERS: Yes, sir.

ALLOTT: Paper: pencils: ink . . . [Sees MOONEY still waiting.] Ipso facto, Mooney.

MOONEY: Yes, sir. [Apprehensive: after exchanging looks with GILLIAN slowly goes.

The others wander off, except CATHERINE, who gets a large drawing-block from her straw bag, and GILLIAN, who has brought her board with her.

STELLA comes on in a dressing-gown.]

STELLA: Thought I'd change in the loo today. Warmer . . . [Shivers: goes to the platform: feels the heater: warms her hands.] Gillian . . . How's Derek?

GILLIAN: All right, Stella.

STELLA: Wish I was young again.

ALLOTT: You are young.

STELLA: Really, youthful young.

ALLOTT: You are youthful young . . . as young as anybody ought to be round here . . . All these aficionados —

myopic . . . disingenuous . . . uninspired – are images of youth no longer: pubescent excrescences on the cheeks of time.

GILLIAN: Oh, sir!

[ALLOTT *has taken the white cloth from the donkey and crosses to the throne.*]

CATHERINE: In any case, study of natural objects isn't very popular today, sir.

ALLOTT: What?

CATHERINE: The study of natural objects.

ALLOTT: Are you a natural object, Stella?

STELLA: Don't feel like one . . . Least, not natural.

CATHERINE: I mean, anything that's real.

ALLOTT: Stella's real . . . Then again, in another sense, you could say she's quite unearthly. [ALLOTT *arranges the white cloth on the throne.*]

CATHERINE: It's more, nowadays, doing what you feel.

ALLOTT: What do you feel, Catherine?

CATHERINE: More expressing . . . sort of . . . whatever it is.

[ALLOTT *waits.*]

Well . . . sort of . . .

[*Waits.*]

I'm speaking, sort of . . . about it all in general.

ALLOTT: I see.

[BRENDA *comes back in with drawing-board, etc.*]

I can't ask Gillian, of course . . . Never known anyone feel so much with so little to show for it – except that unearthly bloody freak.

[MOONEY *is returning with board and paper.*]

CATHERINE: Sir!

BRENDA: She's sensitive, she is . . . aren't you, love?

GILLIAN: Yeh.

BRENDA: She feels it all the time.

GILLIAN: That's right.

MATHEWS [*re-entering*]: Here. Anybody seen my pencil?
[*The girls laugh.*]
Had it in me locker. Pack o'thieves round here . . . Can't put anything down.

BRENDA: No need to look in this direction.

CATHERINE: Accuse anybody, he would.

GILLIAN: Have you looked inside your pockets?

MATHEWS: Want to look in there, then, for me?

GILLIAN: Wouldn't look in there, not if they paid me.

MATHEWS: Not like some of the birds I know.

STELLA: Here, then . . . How do you want me? Standing up today, or sitting down?

ALLOTT: Standing up, I think, to start . . . Recumbent yesterday, I recollect . . . Had the second years in. My God . . . Licentious. To a man.
[MATHEWS *guffaws hugely.*
ALLOTT *circles the platform, chin in hand, contemplating the empty space.*
STELLA *waits.*
CARTER *and* WARREN *have come back in.*]

WARREN: Saw Abercrombie on the stairs . . . come in a bowler hat, he has.

ALLOTT: What's that? [*Studies throne.*]

WARREN: Come in a bowler hat, sir.
[*The girls laugh.*]

ALLOTT: I could do with a bowler hat . . . Gave hints at birthday time . . . what do I get? A box of pencils.

CATHERINE: Artist, sir.

ALLOTT: I have other interests, you know, as well.

MATHEWS: What're they, then, sir? [*He laughs, looking at the others.*]

CARTER: Young ladies.

BRENDA *and* CATHERINE [*together*]: Sir!

163

ALLOTT: Oh, I keep my eye open, Catherine . . not very much here escapes my notice.

GILLIAN: I thought you were married, sir.

ALLOTT: I am married . . . I've been married in fact for a very considerable time . . . In fact, the longer I stay married the more appreciative I become . . .

> Oh, he loved form,
> And he loved beauty –
> But above all else
> He knew his duty.

CATHERINE: Oh, sir!

ALLOTT:
> He called for fruit,
> He called for wine:
> He called for love –
> But that took time.

BRENDA: Go on, sir. That's super.

ALLOTT:
> 'I'll dream of you,' she said:
> *'All life is a fantasy:*
> We create illusions, call them love:'
> Pray sing to me, my dove.

CARTER: Anything else, sir?

ALLOTT: No, no. That's sufficient, I think, to be going on with.

MATHEWS: What other interests have you got, sir?

ALLOTT: Fishing.

MATHEWS: Fishing! [*Laughs.*]

ALLOTT: You interested in fishing, Mathews?

MATHEWS: Not half, sir! [*Laughs.*] Things I go fishing for you don't catch in ponds. [*Laughs.*]

ALLOTT: Where do you catch them, Mathews, if it's not too much to ask?

WARREN: In his bleeding pockets.

CARTER: *Dirty bugger.*

MOONEY: *Dirty sod.*

MATHEWS: Piss off!
  [*The others laugh.*]
ALLOTT: Now, now . . . Stella here's quite shocked . . .
  Never knew they spoke like that, did you, Stell?
STELLA: Hear some things here I'd never hear anywhere
  else.
MATHEWS: Ears like that I'm not surprised.
ALLOTT: Here . . . Here. Now apologize for that. [*Waits.*]
  [*Pause:* MATHEWS *struggles with himself.*]
MATHEWS: I apologize, Stella. Very much.
STELLA: That's all right.
MATHEWS: Give you a kiss, then? Make up.
STELLA: No need to go as far as that, I'm sure.
CARTER: Go a damn sight farther, if he had a chance.
ALLOTT: To your stools, men.
  [*Guffaw from* MATHEWS, CARTER, WARREN.]
  Cathy: close that door. Saunders: let's have the screen to
  stop the draught.
  [*They move to the stools and easels,* CATHERINE *to the
  entrance, stage left,* SAUNDERS *to the screen, centre left:
  arranges it.* STELLA *climbs on to the throne: disrobes.*
  CARTER *whistles.*]
STELLA [*smiles, waiting to be posed*]: Enough. Enough.
WARREN: Why don't you take it off more slowly?
STELLA: Not for you . . . I only do that, you know, for
  friends.
  [*Whistles, catcalls:* ALLOTT *sets the pose: standing.*]
ALLOTT: Left . . . Arm . . . More sort of . . . Right one . . .
  [STELLA *follows his instructions.*]
  That's it . . . Comfortable?
STELLA: Yeh.
  [ALLOTT *chalks her feet: blue chalk which he takes from his
  pocket, marking the white sheet.*]
MATHEWS: Watch your toes, there, darling.

STELLA: Watch your something else, my love.

MATHEWS: Oh. Oh. Hear that . . . Everything's under control. [*Examines his flies.*] Yes . . . yes. Look. Quite nice. Quite lovely.

CARTER: Dirty bugger.

MOONEY: Dirty sod.

ALLOTT: Right, then, Leonardos . . . On your marks, get set . . .

[*MATHEWS blows raspberry.*]

ALLOTT: Go.

[*Laughter: fades slowly:*

they start drawing. SAUNDERS *comes back from setting the screen.* CATHERINE *is already back.*

Each has different mannerisms:

WARREN *stands, straight back, sturdy, draws with charcoal: thick, simple lines: few, much pondered.*

SAUNDERS *uses various aids: hangs plumb-line from strut of stool to squint past: ruler to hold up at arm's length, one eye closed, to gaze at the proportions of Stella: rubber, set-square, penknife: makes numerous dots and marks, as if about to plot a map.*

MATHEWS *draws scruffily, ostentatiously, careless, with numerous scratching movements, scarcely looking at the model, occasionally gasping at errors, or his own perform-ance.*

BRENDA *draws in a similar fashion, but less ostentatiously. Much head-waving from side to side, with odd glances at the model, more to see if she's there, it seems, rather than by way of examination.*

CARTER *stands straight-backed, like Warren, but draws a neat, well-observed, meticulous figure, unimaginative, pains-taking, unengaged.*

CATHERINE *draws in ink: a somewhat dotted figure, like plotting out a graph: much head-waving too, with frequent*

– if brief – glances at Stella: the marks she makes are scarcely visible.

MOONEY *draws an idealized figure: rather like a large banana, smooth, formless, simplified almost to abstraction: studies the model conscientiously.*

GILLIAN *is expressionistic: enjoys drawing: puts a great deal of feeling into it, apparently; yet the result is light, sketchy, almost inconsequential.*

ALLOTT, *after marking off the corners of the cloth on the platform with his blue chalk, walks round a moment, studying the model himself, casually, disinterested.*]

MATHEWS: Here. Go on. Lend us it.

SAUNDERS: Use your own.

MATHEWS: I haven't got one.

ALLOTT: What is it, Marvel?

MATHEWS: Rubber, sir. Saunders. Won't let me have it.

ALLOTT [*looks*]: There's nothing there.

MATHEWS: Is, sir. There, sir.

[ALLOTT *stoops down to* MATHEWS' *drawing from behind* MATHEWS' *back.*]

There.

ALLOTT: Soot.

MATHEWS: No, sir! Made a mistake, sir.

ALLOTT: Lend him it, Saunders. Last time . . . Don't want to see any rubbers after this.

ALL: Oh, sir!

ALLOTT: Draw. Draw. That's all you're here to do.

CARTER: What if we make a mistake, sir?

ALLOTT: Draw round it, underneath it. Makes no difference in the end . . . *What is true will last* . . . What is real – Gillian and Mooney – is eternal.

GILLIAN: Oh, sir.

MATHEWS: Been busy already, hasn't he, Sammy?

[ALLOTT *looks across.*]

Poetical composition, sir.

[WARREN, CARTER, BRENDA *laugh*.]

ALLOTT: Oh time is space

And space is distance,

Distance time

And time consuming . . .

BRENDA: Sir!

ALLOTT: Don't want to see how much, Mathews, just – how well.

MATHEWS: Sir.

ALLOTT: Very nice, Catherine.

CATHERINE: Thank you, sir.

ALLOTT: Fewer calculations, more intuition, Sammy: not a mathematical problem.

SAUNDERS: Yes, sir.

MATHEWS: Mathematical problem to Sammy. Isn't that right?

ALLOTT: Can't draw and talk . . . Can't demonstrate, imbibe, celebrate, Stella's peculiar beauty if you're yakketing all the time.

[ABERCROMBIE *comes in with an electric kettle. Same age as* ALLOTT: *tall, wears a polo-neck sweater, scarf with tassels, gloves, and a bowler hat.*]

ABERCROMBIE: Anybody in?

ALLOTT: Sure.

ABERCROMBIE: Stella.

STELLA: Morning, Mr Abercrombie.

MATHEWS: Morning, Mr Abercrombie.

ABERCROMBIE: Clip your ear, Warren.

MATHEWS: *Mathews*, sir!

ABERCROMBIE: Clip both your ears, Mathews.

MATHEWS: *Sir!*

ABERCROMBIE: Mind if I plug in, old sport?

[ALLOTT *gestures to him to go ahead.*

ABERCROMBIE *glances at the drawings, then at* STELLA, *as he passes: goes to the wall: plugs in kettle.*]

ABERCROMBIE: Damn cold.

ALLOTT: Very.

ABERCROMBIE: Pimples. [*Indicates* STELLA. *To* STELLA] Goose-pimples.

STELLA: All over.

ABERCROMBIE [*to room*]: Don't miss any out.

ALL: Oh, sir.

ABERCROMBIE: How's bis?

ALLOTT: All right.

ABERCROMBIE: Half mine away . . . God. [*Sneezes hugely: produces handkerchief: blows.*]

CATHERINE: Like your hat, sir.

ABERCROMBIE: Thank you, Catherine . . . Lends an air of distinction. [*To* ALLOTT] What d'you think?

ALLOTT: Not seen Philips, have you?

ABERCROMBIE: No . . . [*To* STELLA] Looking your splendid self, my dear.

STELLA: Thank you.

ABERCROMBIE: By God: ten years younger . . . be doing a drawing there meself.

STELLA: Wonder what I'm missing.

ABERCROMBIE: My young days, young lady, wouldn't have to wonder.

STELLA: Ooooh!

ABERCROMBIE: By God. What? . . . Might come in and do an etching . . . Not seen Foley round about?

[ALLOTT *shakes his head.*]

Smell his bloody pipe, but canna see the man. [*Shivers. Slaps his hands together.*] Come cycling in the other morning . . . found Foley parking his car by the rear entrance to the furnace room. Says: 'This area is reserved for artisans, Mr Abercrombie, not for members of the teaching staff.' 'I was parking my bike here, Mr Foley, sir,' I said. 'Bike or no bike, this is for coke, not for members of the staff . . .' gesticulating then to his own automated load of refuse and adding, 'If I leave that on the street I get a parking ticket, so the Principal's car's excluded. All transport apart from that has to find its own parking area. I'd be much obliged.'

ALLOTT: You wheeled it out.

ABERCROMBIE: I rode it into college – left it by his door . . . never said a word . . . made my point. Subsequently hid it discreetly by the furnace . . . where I was this morning when a roar – not unlike a thousand kettles dropped at random by some insidiously careless hand – assailed my ears . . . bob down . . . raise my head . . . cautiously . . . find, though the symphony's subsided, the elements as it were are still around . . . Foley . . . pink-cheeked, per-spiring – *the boot of his car wide open* – stooping to the coke and – not lifting in huge handfuls – but *individual pieces* . . . after which he wipes his hand, lowers the boot, looks round, walks briskly – very much as if he's accomplished a feat of unparalleled dexterity and daring – up the steps to the college entrance.

ALLOTT: What's he want the coke for?

ABERCROMBIE: Fire.

ALLOTT: In his car?

ABERCROMBIE: At home.

ALLOTT: He'll not get much fire with that.

ABERCROMBIE: Suppose he picks up pieces every day . . . after a week . . . a month . . . a year . . . the mind boggles, Allott. He may even, in his leisure hours, run a domestic fuel business . . . his house surrounded by veritable mountains of first-grade coke . . .

[MATHEWS *has had his hand up for several seconds.*]

MATHEWS: Sir? . . .

[ALLOTT *looks up.*]
Can I be excused, sir?

ALLOTT: What for?

MATHEWS [*after some hesitation, and looking round at the others*]: I want to go, sir.

ALLOTT: Where?

MATHEWS: To the bog, sir.

ALLOTT: What do you want to do there?

[*Snort from* WARREN.]

MATHEWS: Sir! I've had some medicine, sir.

ALLOTT: What medicine?

MATHEWS: [*hesitates. Then*]: To make me go, sir.

ALLOTT: Go . . .? You haven't even come.

[*Laughter.*]

MATHEWS: I'll have to go, sir. I've brought a note from my mother.

CARTER: He hasn't got a mother, sir.

MATHEWS: I've got a father.

BRENDA: Different one each day.

MATHEWS: I'll have to go, sir!

MOONEY: Dirty bugger.

WARREN: Dirty sod.

MATHEWS: Sir!

ALLOTT: Two minutes.

MATHEWS: Sir!

ALLOTT: Two minutes.

MATHEWS: *Sir!*

ALLOTT: You can do all you've got to do inside two minutes.

MATHEWS: Sir . . .

[MOONEY *calls to him behind his hand as he passes him to the door.*]
Piss off! [*Goes.*
The room subsides: the students return to work.]

STELLA: There's a draught somewhere.

WARREN: That's Mathews. [*Raspberry.
Laughter.*]

ALLOTT: There's no window open, Stella . . And the door is firmly closed. [*Glances behind screen.*] It is.

STELLA: I can still feel it.

WARREN: What's it feel like, Lovely?

STELLA: Nothing you might mind.

ALLOTT: Where do you feel it, Stella . . .?

STELLA: Sort of . . . down my side.

ALLOTT: Which side?

STELLA: . . . My left side, really.

CARTER: That's not a draught . . . That's Sammy. [*Indicates
SAUNDERS: fixed, scrupulous examination of STELLA.
Laughter.*]

ALLOTT: All right, I'll shift it.

[*Goes to one of two vertical heaters: moves it slightly,
adjusting its position.*]

CATHERINE: Oh, sir!

BRENDA: Oh, *sir*!

CATHERINE: I've drawn it, sir!

BRENDA: *I*'ve drawn it, sir.

ALLOTT: Draw it again.

CATHERINE: I've drawn it *there*, sir!

ALLOTT: Draw it here, then . . . How do you think Degas drew his horses . . . drew his *ballet-dancers*, Catherine?

CATHERINE: Who, sir?

ALLOTT: *Degas*.

GILLIAN: Was he a Negro, Sir?

ALLOTT: No, he wasn't a Negro.

WARREN: Perhaps he took photographs, sir.

ALLOTT: The moving of an electric heater isn't going to jeopardize your drawing unduly . . . [*Looks.*] There's nothing there . . .

172

CATHERINE: There is, sir!

ALLOTT: Shift it.

CATHERINE: Sir: there'll be three of them.

ALLOTT: Better than two . . . [*To* ABERCROMBIE] Most revolutions are the result of quite arbitrary decisions taken, invariably, by people not in the least involved.

WARREN: I wouldn't mind taking one or two snapshots . . . Certain aspects of Stella are very photogenic.

STELLA: Thank you.

ALLOTT [*to* WARREN]: Put away your dirty looks: get on with your dirty drawing.

MOONEY: Got cramp, sir.

ALLOTT: Where?

MOONEY: Finger, sir.

ALLOTT: Massage it.

BRENDA: Ooooh, sir!

CATHERINE: You are awful.

ALLOTT: Get on with it . . .! Drive an angel to distraction . . . Draw, for God's sake, draw!

[*They draw.*]

Your kettle finished?

ABERCROMBIE: Boiled and re-boiled, old boy.

ALLOTT: Saunders, haven't you sharpened that pencil enough by now?

[SAUNDERS *goes on sharpening his pencil: he's been sharpening since* CARTER'*s reference to him.*]

BRENDA: He's crying, sir.

SAUNDERS: I'm not.

CATHERINE: He was, sir . . .

BRENDA: It's what Ken said about him, sir . . .

[GILLIAN *has got up and gone to console* SAUNDERS, *arm round his shoulder.*]

GILLIAN: Oh, you're all right, aren't you, Sammy?

ALLOTT: And what was Carter saying about him?

CATHERINE: About Stella feeling the draught, sir.

ALLOTT: For God's sake, leave him alone, girl . . . Saunders, put your penknife away and draw.

GILLIAN: I was only consoling him, sir.

ALLOTT: You can console him after hours.

BRENDA: *Sir!*

ALLOTT: It's not a clinic, you know. It's not a haven of rest . . . It's where the embryonic artist may experience – perhaps for the very first time in his life, Brenda – the faint flutterings of his restless spirit.

CATHERINE: Oh, sir!

ALLOTT: Get on with it, for Christ's sake.

[GILLIAN *goes back reluctantly to her place.*]
When you've finished picking your nose, Carter, you can go with Mr Abercrombie and ask him for a cup of coffee. I'm parched.

CARTER: Yes, sir.

[*Gets up promptly: waits.*]

ABERCROMBIE: Right . . . [*Hesitates.*] Yes. Well, after all. That's what I came for . . . Kenneth, is it?

CARTER: Yes, sir.

ABERCROMBIE: Right. We'll make Mr Allott's coffee right away . . . Two sugars . . .

ALLOTT: One.

ABERCROMBIE: White . . .

ALLOTT: Black.

ABERCROMBIE [*to* CARTER]: Black. One sugar. [*Goes.*
CARTER *follows.*
Pause. Silence.
MOONEY *whistles a tune contentedly to himself: low, light.*
ALLOTT, *after calming, has begun to wander slowly round the back of the stools, glancing at the drawings.*
Apart from the whistling, the room is silent. Then:]

ALLOTT: Musician.

[*Pause.*]

MOONEY: What?

ALLOTT: Tune.

MOONEY: Oh.

ALLOTT: Preferably silent. [*Indicates the room.*] More creative.

MOONEY: Oh. [*Goes on with his drawing.*
    ALLOTT *gazes at* MOONEY's *drawing. Then:*]

ALLOTT: Draw that with your eyes shut?

MOONEY: What . . .

ALLOTT: Idealized.

MOONEY: What . . .?

ALLOTT: Stella's breasts . . .

ALL: *Ooooh!*

ALLOTT: . . . are not like water melons hanging from a tree.

CATHERINE: Sir!

ALLOTT: They're global masses, but not conceived, as it were, Mooney, on a global scale.

MOONEY: Oh.

ALLOTT: A weight-lifter might find those thighs something of an encumbrance, Mooney . . . It's not a beauty contest, Mooney.

CATHERINE [*having come over to examine the drawing*]: Oooh, sir . . . Honestly!

ALLOTT: Get back to your seat, young woman.

CATHERINE [*returning*]: You ought to see what he's drawn, Jilly.

BRENDA: Better not.

WARREN: Cop a handful of them each evening.

GILLIAN: Shut your mouth.

WARREN: Tits the size of Windsor Castle. [*Standing, peering over.*] Cor blimey . . . get the Eiffel Tower between two o' them.

MOONEY: Piss off.

BRENDA [*to* WARREN]: Upset him.

MOONEY: Piss off you as well.

ALLOTT: It's just a question . . . [*Waits: they quieten, return to drawing.*] It's merely a question, Mooney, of seeing each detail in relation to all the rest . . . When you examine the breasts you've to bear in mind, also, the shape and volume of the head, of the chest structure beneath it, of the abdomen in general . . . the proportion – the width as well as the height – of the legs: the whole contained, as it were . . . [*Looks up: snigger from* WARREN. *Silence. Return to drawing.*] . . . within a single image. Unless you are constantly relating the specific to the whole, Mooney . . . [WARREN *sniggers.*] . . . a work of art can never exist . . . It's not merely a conscious effort; [*Gazing at the others.*] it is, if one is an artist and not merely a technician – someone disguised, that is, as an artist, going through all the motions and creating all the effects – an instinctive process . . . the gift, as it were, of song . . . For, after all, a bird sings in its tree [WARREN *and* BRENDA *snigger.*] but doesn't contemplate its song . . . similarly the artist sings *his* song, but doesn't contemplate its beauty, doesn't analyse, doesn't lay it out in all its separate parts . . . that is the task of the critic, the mechanic . . . even of the poseur, the man masquerading as the artist . . . the *manufacturer* of events who, in his twentieth-century romantic role, sees art as something accessible to all and therefore the prerogative not of the artist – but of anybody who cares to pick up a brush, a bag of cement, an acetylene welder . . . anyone, in fact, who can persuade other people that what he is doing is creative . . . That, after all, is the lesson we must learn, Mooney . . . That's the lesson we've been convened, as it were, to celebrate . . . that we are life's musicians . . .

its singers, and that what we sing is wholly without meaning . . . it exists, merely, because it is . . . The one significant distinction between the artist and the scientist, indeed, between him and all his fellow men . . . What the artist does is purposeless. That's its dignity . . . its beauty.

CATHERINE: I've run out of ink.

ALLOTT: Well, use pencil.

CATHERINE: I've got some in my locker.

ALLOTT: Well, go and get it then.

CATHERINE: Oh, thank you, sir. [Goes quickly.]

WARREN: She's gone for a fag: that's what she's gone for.

ALLOTT: Smoking in the studios, Warren, isn't allowed.

WARREN: She'll smoke it in the bog.

MOONEY: Mr Foley inspects the ladies' lavatories regularly: she'll not smoke anything there.

WARREN: *Dirty bugger.*

MOONEY: *Dirty sod.*

ALLOTT: Commemoration of the human spirit and human hygiene often go hand in hand, Mooney.

MOONEY: It wasn't me, sir. It was him.

ALLOTT: Human hygiene and commemoration of the human spirit often go hand in hand, Warren.

WARREN: Yes, sir.

ALLOTT: Did you get that, Warren?

WARREN: Yes, sir.

ALLOTT: I'd hate you to overlook it.

WARREN: Yes, sir.

ALLOTT [*to* GILLIAN]:

> Oh, love will run its course,
> Come finally to rest,
> And panting, reined in,
> Stand waiting for its test.

GILLIAN: Super, sir!

ALLOTT: Thank you, Gillian.

CATHERINE [*returning, breathless*]: Got it, sir. [*Begins drawing immediately.*]

ALLOTT [*to* WARREN]: Ink is what she wanted: ink is what she got.

WARREN: Yes, sir.

ALLOTT: A man's faith, Warren, is seldom easily come by.

WARREN: No, sir.

ALLOTT: The greatest harm one human being can do to another is to seek to disillusion him . . . some people take longer, for instance, to fill their pens than others.

WARREN: Yes sir.

ALLOTT: And some, of course, never need to fill their pens at all.

WARREN: No, sir.

[MOONEY *and* BRENDA *snigger.*]

ALLOTT: Is that a mystery figure, Brenda? . . . Have we – at the end of the day – to decide what it is, where it came from, and who its antecedents are?

BRENDA: No, sir.

ALLOTT: Unformed. Wouldn't you say that's a reasonable assessment, Brenda?

BRENDA: No, sir.

ALLOTT: What Mooney's has got a superabundance of, yours has got none at all.

CATHERINE: It's different for a girl, sir.

ALLOTT: How do you mean?

CATHERINE: Well, sir . . .

BRENDA: Drawing breasts, sir.

GILLIAN: Yeh.

CATHERINE: It's different for a girl.

BRENDA: If we'd got a feller to draw it'd be different, sir.

CATHERINE: We could get going with a feller, sir.

WARREN: Hang one on him three feet long.

MOONEY: *Dirty bugger.*

WARREN: *Dirty sod.*

ALLOTT: Warren – *if* you're doing anything at all, that is – it's of far greater interest to me than any of these diverting comments you feel constrained to make from time to time. [*Waits.*] Get on with it.

WARREN: It's sexual discrimination, sir.

ALLOTT: There's no sexual discrimination here . . . Art is above sex . . . and it's above politics, too. That's to say, it absorbs sex, and it absorbs politics.

BRENDA: Why're we always drawing women, then?

ALLOTT: You're not always drawing women.

GILLIAN: We are in here.

CATHERINE: That's sexual discrimination. That's what I mean.

ALLOTT: We had a man once. I remember distinctly.

WARREN: Gave 'em all a shock, sir . . . Shoulda seen it. Almost to his knee-caps, sir.

GILLIAN: S'only nature.

CATHERINE: Yeh. It's only nature.

BRENDA: That's what I mean . . . Just once.

ALLOTT: We're not here to seek sexual stimulation, Catherine. We're here to peruse a beautiful and seemingly mysterious object, and to set it down – curiously – as objectively as we can.

BRENDA: It's alus a woman, sir.

SAUNDERS: Women have always been the subject of the very greatest art.
   [*Pause: they look at* SAUNDERS.]
Because all the greatest artists, you see, have always been men.

GILLIAN: We know why, don't we, Sammy?

ALLOTT: I don't know why. Have you some information on the subject you've been keeping back from us, Jilly?

GILLIAN: They like contemplating their human slaves.

WARREN: What slaves?

SAUNDERS: Who's a slave?

GILLIAN: Us. We're slaves.

MOONEY: Who keeps you in slavery?

GILLIAN: You do.

MOONEY: Me?

CATHERINE: *Men.*

WARREN: Bollocks.

GILLIAN: That's a man's answer to everything . . . *Bollocks.*

MOONEY: I don't like women swearing . . . I've told you that before.

GILLIAN: Piss off!

BRENDA: Ooooh, Jilly!

WARREN: They're a pain in the arse, sir. They are, honestly.

SAUNDERS: If women wanted to be artists they've more time than anybody else.

BRENDA: Rubbish . . .

CATHERINE: Bollocks!

[*The girls laugh.*]

WARREN: Cor blimey . . . sat on their backsides all day at home . . . if they wanted to paint bloody pictures they'd find the time, don't worry.

GILLIAN: That's what you know. That's all you think.

WARREN: Cor blimey . . . bored out of their minds, middle-class women.

SAUNDERS: Look at the rich, well-to-do women in the nineteenth century.

WARREN: Tell me they haven't had the opportunity or the time . . .

SAUNDERS: As for the men . . .

WARREN: Work their bollocks off feeding a bloody family, *then* come home and create a work of art . . . you don't know when you're well off.

BRENDA: Piss off.

WARREN: You piss off.

CATHERINE: You piss off.

WARREN: And *you* piss off.

ALLOTT: Discussions of this sort invariably serve a useful function, clarifying the issues, setting them, if anything, in a wider context, removing the edge of personal, not to say sexual, vindictiveness . . .

WARREN [*to* BRENDA]: Get this up your nose you'd piss off all right.

BRENDA: Get this somewhere else and you'd piss off all right.

ALLOTT: The education of the working class of course is still something of an anomaly.

WARREN [*to* BRENDA]: Bollocks!

BRENDA: Bollocks.

WARREN: You haven't got no bollocks.

BRENDA: Neither have you!

[*Laughter from the girls.*]

ALLOTT: You could say that women have never had the *consciousness* to become artists – there are exceptions but I mean as a general rule.

WARREN: Yeh, but, sir . . .

SAUNDERS: I mean, don't you think that it would be extraordinary, Mr Allott, that something that has been denied women for so long should have taken all this time to emerge – I mean, their natural but frustrated capacity to be great thinkers, great composers, great artists, great poets . . . great originators of thought and feeling? It seems humanly impossible that if this is an intrinsic part of the female temperament it should never have shown itself in any of these forms.

CATHERINE: Yeh . . . but that's the point, i'n it? In women it's been made *unnatural*.

WARREN: Piss off.

CATHERINE: You piss off!

BRENDA: Whose side are you on, sir?

ALLOTT: Nobody's. That's to say, I'm accepting that anything is possible, but that for now, at this minute, Stella is standing there, in all her pristine glory . . .

STELLA: I've got pins and needles.

ALLOTT: Whether women have been the object – or even the subject – of men's abuse, she is – and I insist that you still see her as – a human being. And it's as a human being you'll draw her, and it's as a human being you'll record your impressions of her . . . insufferable to look at as some of those impressions well may be.

STELLA: Can I have a rest?

ALLOTT: No.

GILLIAN: Sir!

ALLOTT: She's always trying to get round me.

CATHERINE: Sir!

ALLOTT: If she's really got pins and needles she'd have collapsed already. Can you feel a draught?

STELLA: No.

ALLOTT: Right, then.

MATHEWS [*entering*]: Those bogs want cleaning out.
    [*Laughter.*]

GILLIAN: After you've been in, especially.

MATHEWS: *Afore* I went in . . . That caretaker never goes in there. Sweeps to the bloody door then stops.

WARREN: What are you, Mathews, man or woman?

MATHEWS: If you've two minutes to step outside I'll show you.

WARREN: I mean in the political contest between the sexes, Bryan. Are you a man or are you a woman?

MATHEWS: I'm a woman. I'm on the woman's side in everything.

MOONEY: Front and back, an' all: it makes no difference to Mathews.

MATHEWS [*makes a fist*]: You'll get this under your fucking nose.

BRENDA: How did your medicine work, then? Long and easy?

MATHEWS: And up yours . . . I'm not above using this, you know.

WARREN: But slowly. Each evening, tha knows, afore he goes to bed.

[*Laughter from the girls.*]

MATHEWS: Piss off.

CATHERINE, GILLIAN *and* BRENDA [*together*]: *Piss off!* [*They laugh.*]

ALLOTT: Coffee time, nearly. [*Examines his watch: winds it.*]

BRENDA: Aren't you going to do any drawing, sir?

ALLOTT: I might . . . I might. [*Examines watch again.*] This time of the day the mind unfolds . . . my time of life, however, Brenda, inspiration often falters.

CATHERINE: What about us, then, sir?

ALLOTT: I was coming to you, Catherine, as a matter of fact . . . These invisible compositions . . . You look [*Indicates* STELLA.] . . . Examine . . . Set down . . . But I'm damned if I can find a mark.

CATHERINE: There, sir.

ALLOTT: Where . . .?

CATHERINE: Head . . . arms . . . legs . . . feet.

ALLOTT: What's that?

CATHERINE: Her head, sir.

ALLOTT: It's a piece of fluff. [*Brushes it off with his hand.*] No it's not.

CATHERINE: It's her head, sir.

ALLOTT: What's this?

CATHERINE: Her breast, sir.

WARREN, MATHEWS *and* MOONEY [*together*]: *Ooooh!*

ALLOTT: Where's the other one?

WARREN: She hasn't got one.

   [*Laughter.*]

CATHERINE: I haven't done it, sir.

ALLOTT: There are two of these objects . . . perhaps you haven't noticed. And good grief. This other bit of fluff . . .

CATHERINE: I was pin-pointing the principal masses, sir.

ALLOTT: You've been stabbing them to death. Just look at this.

   [MATHEWS, *rising, has leaned over to look.*]

MATHEWS: One tit, one cunt: that's all she's got.

ALLOTT: [*straightens: surveys* MATHEWS *for a moment. Then*]: I know your personality hasn't a great deal to recommend it, Mathews; but what little charm it does possess is scarcely enhanced by a remark like that . . . If you could just concentrate on the job in hand.

WARREN: He hasn't got it in hand, sir; that's his trouble.

ALLOTT: The object, Mathews. The thing you see before you . . . I take it that's your latest design for a coal-mine, Warren.

WARREN: Sir?

ALLOTT: Is there a human being lying somewhere under that?

WARREN: It's very difficult to concentrate here, sir.

ALLOTT: Michelangelo lay on his back all day to paint the Sistine ceiling . . . he drew on his inner resources, Warren . . . brought them up from deep inside.

   [MATHEWS *belches.*]

Unaided, even, by patent laxative. [*Returns to* CATHERINE.] The problem, Catherine . . . isn't to pin-point . . . nor even to isolate . . . it's to incorporate everything that is happening out there into a single homogeneous whole.

CATHERINE [*gazing at* STELLA]: There's nothing happening, sir.

ALLOTT: There's a great deal happening . . . Not in any obvious way . . . nevertheless several momentous events are actually taking place out there . . . subtly, quietly, not overtly . . . but in the way that artistic events *do* take place . . . in the great reaches of the mind . . . the way the leg, for instance, articulates with the hip, the shoulders with the thorax; the way the feet display the weight . . . the hands subtended at the end of either arm . . . these are the wonders of creation, Catherine . . . Is your pen absolutely full? [*Has taken it to indicate the parts of the drawing to her: no mark. Shakes it down violently.*]

CATHERINE: Sir: you've blotted!

ALLOTT: Blots are indicative of industry, Catherine. Of energy. Passion. Draw round it. [*Rises, handing the pen to her.*]

WARREN: Could make it into your pubic, Cathy.

CATHERINE: Piss off.

WARREN: You piss off as well.

CARTER [*entering with cup and saucer*]: Coffee up, sir.

ALLOTT: Not before time.

BRENDA: Rest, sir?

ALLOTT: The model is there, Brenda, for your edification. She's not a motif. Your glances in her direction – few and far between – are to reassure yourself she's still in the room. She is there to be examined . . . If only at a distance, Carter.

[STELLA *has whispered to* CARTER, 'Any for me?'; *he's gone nearer to answer.*]

ALLOTT: . . . If only at a distance, Carter.

CARTER: I didn't say anything, sir.

ALLOTT: Coffee cold?

CARTER: No, sir. It's just been made.

ALLOTT: I don't want to find anything in the saucer.

CARTER: No, sir.

ALLOTT: Hold it straight. [*To* MATHEWS] I'm not sure what comment I can make on Mathews' . . . An advertisement, perhaps, for rubber tyres . . . [*Twists his head.*] Or the effect of too much alcohol on the human brain . . . [*Twists his head again.*] Burnt porridge, emerging through a Scotch mist . . . at three, perhaps three-thirty of a winter's morn . . .

MATHEWS: I've not had time to get started, sir.

ALLOTT: That's what I mean . . . The whole process, Mathews, has not begun: mass before beauty, excrescence before edification . . . salaciousness before refinement . . . Has anyone here seen Mr Philips?

BRENDA: No, sir.

GILLIAN: No, sir.

WARREN: No, sir.

MATHEWS: Got something on, then, have you?

ALLOTT: What?

[MATHEWS *makes the sound of a galloping horse, clicking his tongue against his teeth – and holding a pair of invisible reins, urgently, in his hands.*]

You still taking that medicine, Mathews?

MATHEWS: No, sir.

ALLOTT: Better get downstairs . . . and take another dose. *Rest!*

[*Laughter: scramble for the door.*

STELLA *descends, stretching.*]

BRENDA: How long we got, sir?

ALLOTT: As long as I tell you.

WARREN: Watch it, Stella. [*Grapples with her.*]

STELLA: Get off, you filthy-minded beast.

[MATHEWS *blows raspberry: they all go, but for* SAUN-

186

DERS: *after getting up slowly, even reluctantly, he wanders round the drawings, examining.*]

ALLOTT: Going for a cup of tea, Samuel?

SAUNDERS: Yes, sir . . . [*Casual*] Stella? You going?

STELLA: I'll be along in a minute, love . . . My back . . . Can you see anything on it? [*Turns it to* ALLOTT.]

ALLOTT: Here?

STELLA: No . . .

ALLOTT: Here?

STELLA: Here . . .

ALLOTT: What sort of thing?

STELLA: Knocked it . . . when I got up it was terribly stiff . . . I'll be along in a jiffy, Sammy.

SAUNDERS [*who's been waiting*]: Oh . . . all right. [*Glances at her: goes.*]

STELLA: Been measuring me again.

ALLOTT: Who?

STELLA: Sammy . . . Look at all these plumb-lines . . . Anybody'd think he was going to reconstruct me . . . build me in concrete somewhere else.

ALLOTT: Your statistics are of immeasurable significance to him, Stella . . . I can't see anything at all.

STELLA: You coming, are you? [*Puts on her dressing-gown.* CATHERINE *has come back in.*]

ALLOTT: No, no. I'll drink it here.

STELLA: See you. [*Goes.*
CATHERINE *has gone to throne, sat down with her straw bag: gets out flask, sandwiches: pours tea.*
ALLOTT *watches her. Then:*]

ALLOTT: Cucumber?

CATHERINE: Lettuce.

ALLOTT: Looks just like cucumber from over here.

CATHERINE: Lettuce.

ALLOTT: Don't you eat anything else?

CATHERINE: Haven't got time.

ALLOTT: My wife is coming up today.

CATHERINE: Is she, sir? What for?

ALLOTT: We've been separated, you know, for some considerable time. She's coming, I suspect, to give me news of a very significant nature . . . or, in the terminology of the employment exchange, my cards.

CATHERINE: Oh, I'm sorry, sir.

ALLOTT: One of those things. The artist, after all, has no real life outside his work. Whenever he attempts it, the results, Catherine, leave – to say the very least of it – a great deal to be desired . . . Refreshing.

CATHERINE: Yes, sir?

ALLOTT: Cucumber . . . Don't you find it refreshing?

CATHERINE: Have one, sir, if you want.

ALLOTT: No. No . . . I couldn't eat a thing.

CATHERINE: What sort of pictures do you paint, sir?

ALLOTT: I don't.

CATHERINE: Do you do sculpture, then?

ALLOTT: No. [*Shakes his head.*]

CATHERINE: What do you do, then, sir?

ALLOTT: It's my opinion that painting and sculpture, and all the traditional forms of expression in the plastic arts, have had their day, Catherine . . . It's my opinion that the artist has been driven back – or driven on, to look at it in a positive way – to creating his works, as it were, in public.

CATHERINE: In public, sir?

ALLOTT: Just as Courbet or Modigliani, or the great Dutch Masters . . . created their work out of everyday things, so the contemporary artist creates his work out of the experience – the events as well as the objects – with which he's surrounded in his day-to-day existence . . . for instance, our meeting here today . . . the feelings and intuitions expressed by all of us inside this room . . . are in effect the creation – the re-creation – of the artist . . . to the extent that they are controlled, manipulated, postulated, processed, defined, sifted, re*fined* . . .

CATHERINE: Who by, sir?

ALLOTT: Well, for want a better word – by me.

[*Pause.*]

CATHERINE: Oh.

FOLEY [*entering*]: Has somebody been bloody well smoking in here?

[FOLEY *is a bluff, red-faced man, an embryonic wrestler in physique: about fifty to fifty-five.*]

ALLOTT [*standing immediately*]: No.

FOLEY [*gazing round. Then*]: Who?

CATHERINE [*rising abruptly*]: Catherine, sir.

FOLEY: Pipe tobacco . . . they can't even be honest about it and smoke a cigarette . . . Think it'll get wafted up with my own . . . Think, you know, that a smoker can't smell his own tobacco. I'm different in that respect . . . Who?

CATHERINE: Catherine, sir.

FOLEY: What?

CATHERINE: Smith, sir.

FOLEY: Any relation to Walter Smith?

CATHERINE: No, sir.

FOLEY: Walter Smith's a very fine window cleaner. Cleans my windows a treat. Where's everybody gone?

ALLOTT: Rest.

FOLEY: What's this? [WARREN's *drawing.*]

ALLOTT: He's breaking it down, I believe . . . into its individual masses.

FOLEY: Crushing it to bloody death, it seems to me. [*Turns the drawing upside down.*] The Black Hole of Calcutta . . . See it? . . . All those figures? . . . And that man trying to claw his way towards the light . . .

ALLOTT: Yes.

FOLEY: I should suggest he starts on it upside down.

ALLOTT: Yes.

FOLEY: What's this . . .? [*Peers closely at* CATHERINE's.]

ALLOTT: That's Catherine's, as a matter of fact.

FOLEY: Sat here all morning doing nowt, then.

ALLOTT: There are one or two marks . . . indicative of the principal masses.

FOLEY: T'ony thing I can see is a bloody blot . . . Doesn't take long to draw a blot . . . This the pen you use, then, is it? . . . You don't want to use ought automatic when you turn to art . . . automatic pens are out . . . plastic paraphernalia that no artist of any note has any time for . . . Sithee [*To* ALLOTT]: when you set a pose, you want to set a teaser . . . summat'll stretch em out . . . arm up here . . . leg out . . . hip thrust in opposite direction [*Shows him.*] . . . All this straight up and down nonsense, I reckon nowt to that . . . The model doesn't smoke, then, does she?

ALLOTT: I'm not sure.

FOLEY [*looks behind screen*]: Where's her undies?

ALLOTT: She changes in the ladies . . . warmer.

FOLEY: No relation to Gordon Smith?

CATHERINE: No, sir.

FOLEY: Seen Philips, have you? [*Going.*]

ALLOTT: I was looking for him myself.

FOLEY: Think on: arm up, leg out. Get summat classical, tha knows. [*Goes.*

CATHERINE *sighs. Sits down.*

ALLOTT *sits too, after a moment.*]

CATHERINE: I didn't see you doing much controlling there, sir.

ALLOTT: I wouldn't agree with you entirely, Catherine . . . Silence can guide, you know, as well as absorb.

CATHERINE: I don't think anyone guides Mr Foley.

ALLOTT: There are certain ungovernables in life, but even they can be incorporated into a general pattern – into a single, coherent whole . . . other things, of course, don't have to be guided.

CATHERINE: Such as, sir?

ALLOTT: Natural impulses. Feeling creates its own form, form its own feeling.

CATHERINE: I'm not sure what you mean there, sir.

ALLOTT: Who can distinguish between the feeling, for instance, that informs a shape, and the shape itself? The one is a natural concomitant of the other . . . indistinguishable. Inseparable.

[*Waits.*]

Then again, in personal feelings who's to say that what one feels for an individual can ever be separated from how they look, or are, or indeed, as the phrase goes, have their being? I have my feelings about you, Catherine, and I associate them, irretrievably, with your appearance – how you walk, and speak . . . is that your hat?

CATHERINE: I brought it this morning to show to Brenda.

ALLOTT: It's very becoming . . .

[CATHERINE *puts it on, unselfconscious.*

ALLOTT *watches.*]

Really . . .

CATHERINE: Do you like it?

ALLOTT: It's very beautiful . . .

[CATHERINE *turns her head.*]

What could be simpler . . . I really think . . . well. It's very charming.

[*Pause.*

WARREN *puts his head round the screen from the door.*]

WARREN: Foley's looking for a smoker . . . In the women's

bogs. Asked me if there was anyone I knew who smoked a pipe.

CATHERINE: He does.

WARREN: 'You, sir.' That's what I said. *He* said: 'None of your bloody cheek, Carter, or I'll clip you round the head.' I said, 'My name's Warren, sir.' He said, 'Well, I'll clip Warren round the head,' and added, after a moment's reflection, *threateningly*, 'You can tell him that from me.' [*To* CATHERINE] Was Saunders crying?

CATHERINE: Course he was . . .

WARREN: Poorly, is he?

CATHERINE: He's in love with Stella.

WARREN: Can't be.

CATHERINE: Can't see why not.

ALLOTT: Artists have frequently been known to fall in love with the subject of their art.

WARREN: Not Saunders. He can't look at a tit without getting out a ruler.

ALLOTT: Perhaps it's the wrong instrument, but the instinct, I'm sure, is still the same.

WARREN: Who'd have believed it?

CATHERINE: I'll go and put my hat in the locker. It might get damaged up here.

WARREN: Might get nicked. [*Gesturing off.*]

CATHERINE: The women you can trust here, Warren. [*Goes.* WARREN *wanders aimlessly round the drawings. Then:*]

WARREN: You go in for all this art, then, sir?

ALLOTT: It's a job . . .

WARREN: Doesn't seem real, somehow.

ALLOTT: We all sail, to some extent, under false colours, Warren . . . I mean, you may not see yourself as an artist . . . I may not see myself as a teacher . . . No one of any consequence paints the human figure, for instance, any more . . . it's not even a discipline because, if you

presented me with a straight line and told me that's what
you saw – under the absurd licence of modern illusionism
– I'd have to accept it. Stella earns her living; I earn my
living . . . you earn your living – a mere pittance, I agree
– one of the world's exploited . . . but between us, we
convene . . . celebrate . . . initiate . . . an event, which,
for me, is the very antithesis of what *you* term reality . . .
namely we embody, synthesize, evoke, a work, which,
whether we are aware of it nor not, is taking place around
us . . . [*Indicates* SAUNDERS' *entrance.*] all the time.

> [WARREN *watches* SAUNDERS, *who makes no gesture to
> them: he crosses to the throne, sits there, on the edge, away
> from them. Then:*]

WARREN: All right, Sammy?

SAUNDERS: Yeh.

WARREN [*looking at* SAUNDERS' *drawing*]: Not got much
done for a morning.

SAUNDERS: No.

WARREN: Still . . . Plenty of time yet, Sam.

SAUNDERS: Yeh.

> [CARTER *enters: eyes on* SAUNDERS: *evidently been follow-
> ing him outside. He's followed in by* MATHEWS, *eyes on*
> SAUNDERS *too.*]

CARTER: How's Sammy?

SAUNDERS: All right.

MATHEWS: Cleared up, has it?

SAUNDERS: What?

MATHEWS: Eye . . .

SAUNDERS: Yeh.

MATHEWS: Lot o' dust . . . [*Wafts round.*] . . . can see it
circling . . . [*Gazes up, following it with finger.*] Ooh!
[*Clutches his eye.*]

WARREN: What's all this?

CARTER: Tell you later.

MATHEWS [*to* WARREN]: S-a-m invited Stella out tonight.

SAUNDERS: What's Stella say?

MATHEWS *and* CARTER [*together*]: *Piss off!* [*They laugh.*
SAUNDERS *gets up: finds nowhere to go: goes to donkey:
strips sheet of paper from his board. Sits.*]

WARREN: Mr Foley's been looking for a pipe-smoker,
Sammy.

SAUNDERS: Has he?

WARREN: Got his suspicions.

MATHEWS: Came out of the women's bog.

CARTER: Dirty bugger . . .

MATHEWS: Dirty sod!

WARREN: She was only an artist's daughter . . .

MATHEWS: But she knew where to draw the line.

[*Laughter.*]

CARTER: Going, sir?

[ALLOTT *has made a move for the door.*]

ALLOTT: Yes . . . I shan't be a moment . . . Paper . . .
Pen . . . [*Feels in his pockets.*] Ah, yes. Here we are.
[*Goes.*]

CARTER: Diarrhoea!

WARREN: Constipation!

MATHEWS: Poetry coming on!

[*They laugh.*]

WARREN: Why's he teach in this pissed-off dump?

SAUNDERS: Van Gogh couldn't even get a job.

MATHEWS: Who's Van Gogh?

[*Laughter.*]

SAUNDERS: Don't judge people by appearances; that's all,
Warren.

CARTER: That's your considered opinion is it, Sammy?

SAUNDERS: It's not considered. It's just a simple fact of life.

MATHEWS: You know a lot about life then, Sammy.

SAUNDERS: I don't know much at all, as a matter of fact. I know something about Mr Allott, though.

CARTER: What?

SAUNDERS: That he's sincere in his beliefs.

WARREN: Is he?

[SAUNDERS *doesn't answer.*]

MATHEWS: What beliefs are those, when they're all at home?

SAUNDERS: Perhaps there isn't a role left for the artist . . . perhaps, in an egalitarian society – so-called – an artist is a liability . . . after all, he's an individual: he tells you by his gift alone that all people can't be equal . . . why should one person have a beautiful voice if we can't all have it . . .? That's what it's coming to . . . That's an opinion, however, not a fact of life.

CARTER: Why go on measuring up all these beautiful women, Sammy?

SAUNDERS: There's something dispassionate in human nature . . . that's what I think . . . something really dispassionate that nothing – no amount of pernicious and cruel experience – can ever destroy. That's what I believe in . . . I think a time will come when people will be interested in what was dispassionate at a time like this . . . when everything was dictated to by so much fashion . . . by fashion and techniques.

WARREN: You draw like a machine: what you worrying about?

SAUNDERS: I use a bit of string, and a stone. If I can't measure what I see how can I relate it?

WARREN: Silly prick.

CARTER: He talks like Allott.

WARREN: He looks like Allott.

MATHEWS: He smells like Allott.

CARTER, WARREN *and* MATHEWS [*together*]: *He is Allott!*
[*They laugh.*
    BRENDA *comes in.*]
BRENDA: Have we started?
CARTER: Not yet, my darling. [*Embraces her.*]
BRENDA: Get off . . . [*Stays in his embrace, however.*] That
coffee does terrible things to your stomach.
MATHEWS: Come a bit closer and I might do something
better.
BRENDA: Piss off. [*Sways with* CARTER *in embrace.*]
WARREN: I don't think women should swear, as a matter of
fact.
MATHEWS: Neither do I.
BRENDA: Why not?
WARREN: I'll tell you why . . . I've never heard *one* who can
do it with conviction.
BRENDA: Fuck off.
WARREN [*to* CARTER]: There's a first time, you see, for
everything.
    [CATHERINE *enters, gasping.*]
CATHERINE: Have we started?
BRENDA: No, love. [*Kissing* CARTER, *in whose arms she still
sways.*]
CATHERINE: Once up and down the stairs . . . [*Collapses on
donkey.*]
WARREN: Why d'you do it, Catherine?
CATHERINE: Get varicose veins, you know, with sitting.
MATHEWS: I could give you all the exercise you want.
CATHERINE: So I've heard.
WARREN: Follows you up and down, he does.
CARTER: Stairs . . .
WARREN: Likes the colour of your knickers.
CATHERINE: That's as close as he'll ever get.

MATHEWS: I think women ought to wear trousers, as a matter of fact.

BRENDA: Why?

[CARTER *has already released her.*]

MATHEWS: Look silly wearing skirts. Men don't show off their underwear, do they?

BRENDA: Not your dirty, filthy, bloody stuff.

MATHEWS: Piss off.

WARREN: Get your hand in easier, Bryan. [*Gropes* BRENDA.]

MATHEWS: Yeh . . . Hadn't thought of that!

BRENDA: Piss off.

WARREN: Piss off yourself . . . [*Raspberry.*

MATHEWS *joins* WARREN *with* BRENDA: *they fight.* PHILIPS *enters.*]

PHILIPS [*briskly*]: Morning, boys . . . Mr Allott about, then, is he? . . . Morning, ladies.

[PHILIPS *is a small, dapper, military figure, stiff, between forty and fifty: he bows to the two girls as the fighting subsides.*]

WARREN: He's popped out for a moment, Mr Philips.

PHILIPS: By God, rest time, is it?

CARTER: Yes, sir.

MATHEWS: Was there any message in particular you wanted passing on, sir?

PHILIPS [*crossing to throne and heaters*]: Lovely and warm in here . . . Warmest room in the building.

WARREN: We're about to start any minute, sir.

PHILIPS: I'll hang on. I'll hang on. [*Warms his hands at the heater.*] By God: tempted to become a model, you know, myself.

CARTER: Is it true at one time, sir, you were an amateur boxer? [*Glancing at the others.*]

PHILIPS: That's quite correct.

CARTER: Lightweight, sir?

PHILIPS: Oh, one of the lightweight categories, you can be
sure of that . . .

WARREN: Still in good shape, sir.

PHILIPS: I could give a round or two to some of these
youngsters nowadays . . . Two days of roadwork and
they want to turn professional . . . By God, some of the
best boxers of the day, you know, were amateur . . .
never stepped inside a professional ring. Knew what the
business was all about and had their priorities in the
proper order. The moment sport and money mix, the
former – you can take it from me – goes out of the
window.

STELLA [*entering*]: Time is it?

PHILIPS: My God, and come out fighting! [*Dances forward,
fists ready: laughs.*]

STELLA: Oh, Mr Philips . . .

PHILIPS: Up on your throne, young lady. Give it all you've
got . . . Come on, come on, there. Mr Allott can't be far
away, I can tell you that.

[*They go slowly to their respective easels and donkeys.*
SAUNDERS, *who has been sharpening his pencil since his
last dialogue, has attached a fresh sheet of paper to his
drawing-board.*
STELLA *mounts the platform.*]

Few masterpieces I can see already on the way . . . Might
turn that into a lithograph, Carter . . . one or two nice
textures there . . .

CARTER: That's Warren's.

PHILIPS: All true art is impersonal. Who said that?

MATHEWS: Mr Allott, sir.

PHILIPS [*pause. Then*]: That's quite correct.

STELLA: Well . . . Are you ready?

WARREN: Ready.

MATHEWS: Ready.

CARTER: Ready.

STELLA: For *drawing*.

WARREN: Mr Philips is dying for a look . . .

PHILIPS: Oh, I've seen plenty of models in my time, I can tell you that . . . Those of us in the Design Department aren't that far removed from life . . . Now, what's the pose . . .? Chalk marks all correct?

[PHILIPS *stands by the throne.*

STELLA *removes her robe.*

PHILIPS *gazes at her.*]

Left . . . more left . . . [*Glances at one of the drawings.*] Right hand . . . That's correct . . . [*Looks round.*] Everyone satisfied?

WARREN: If you are, sir.

PHILIPS: Oh, I'm satisfied . . . I'm satisfied well enough . . . Catherine, my dear?

CATHERINE: Yes, sir.

PHILIPS: Brenda?

BRENDA: Yes, sir.

[*They all begin.*

They work in silence: gradually, one by one, heads turn and gaze at SAUNDERS *who, solemnly, has begun his measuring out and his careful drawing. After a while the whole room's attention is on him, even finally* STELLA *herself, who, without moving her body, turns her head and looks.*

SAUNDERS, *aware of her gaze, looks up.*

PHILIPS, *who has been inspecting the girls' drawings from behind their backs, looks up too.*]

PHILIPS: Is anything the matter?

WARREN: No, sir.

MATHEWS: No, sir.

CARTER: No, sir.

BRENDA: No, sir.

CATHERINE: No, sir.

PHILIPS: Well, then . . . get on with it.

    [*They begin again. After a while the heads begin to turn again: finally they all gaze at* SAUNDERS.

    SAUNDERS, *drawing, becomes aware of their fresh scrutiny. After a moment's hesitation he gets up: takes up his plumb-line, his various pieces, his board, his paper.*

    GILLIAN *and* MOONEY *come in as* SAUNDERS *leaves. He brushes past them, goes.*]

MOONEY: What's up with Sammy, then?

CARTER: Love-sick.

WARREN: Silly pillock.

    [MATHEWS *blows raspberry.*]

GILLIAN: Hello, Mr Philips.

MOONEY: Filling in . . .?

PHILIPS: Temporary absence of Mr Allott . . . And which is your drawing, my dear?

GILLIAN: This one.

PHILIPS: Delicate . . . very delicate. [*Examines it, then indicates* STELLA.] You'll notice . . . [*Crosses to* STELLA.] the thigh . . . [*Runs his hand along it.*] is relaxed when the weight is on the other foot . . . it's suspended from the pelvis . . . here . . . at a lower point than where – because it's taking the weight – it's *inserted* on the other side . . . [*Demonstrates with both hands.*]

GILLIAN: Yes.

PHILIPS: The hips, therefore, represent something of an acute angle, subtended from the horizontal.

WARREN: He's not going to grope her, is he?

PHILIPS: Have I made it clear?

GILLIAN: Yes, sir.

    [PHILIPS *moves back to the drawing: walks around the rear of the students: leans over one or two boys.*]

PHILIPS [*to* CARTER]: More . . . That's better . . . [*Points it*

out on the paper. Moves on. To WARREN] Clearer . . .
clearer . . . A good clean line . . . [*To* MATHEWS, *after a
quick perusal and passing on*] That's coming on . . .
 [*Work in silence for a while.*
 In silence ALLOTT *enters: unnatural: looks round. Pause.
 Then:*]

ALLOTT: Where's Saunders, then?

CARTER: Love-sick, sir.

PHILIPS: Temporarily absented . . . One or two nice
effects . . . [*Indicates students' work.*]

ALLOTT: Blue Moon came up at Kempton.

PHILIPS: Do you want it in tens or fives?

ALLOTT: It always feels much better in shillings. [*Holds out
his hand.*]
 [PHILIPS *sorts coins: hands them over.*]
Looked for you all over this morning.

PHILIPS: Dear boy: I've only just arrived.

ALLOTT: You don't understand, Philips. This is the first
time I've ever won.

PHILIPS: Incredible, old boy . . . No, no. really. [*Sorts last
coin: hands it over.*]

ALLOTT [*gazing up*]: Somewhere, in that indefinable
miasma we call life, there's some creature looking
down . . . 'Allott,' it said. 'Allott . . . Let Allott win the
four-fifteen.'

PHILIPS: Nearly the three o'clock as well.

ALLOTT: That was a different matter entirely.

PHILIPS: I said go for a place, old boy.

ALLOTT: I just felt that fate had bigger things in store.

PHILIPS: It had. It had.

ALLOTT [*gazes at the coins in his hand. Then*]: I'd almost
given up hope, Philips.

PHILIPS: Don't give up hope, old boy . . . After all, what're we in this business for . . . No. This. [*Indicates the model, room.*]

ALLOTT: Ah . . . Yes.

PHILIPS: Posterity, old son. If they don't see it now they'll see it later. We're building up an enormous credit . . . [*Gestures aimlessly overhead.*] somewhere . . . You with your . . . events . . . me with my designs . . . book-jackets, posters . . . Letraset . . . singular embodiments of the age we live in.

ALLOTT: Sold anything lately?

PHILIPS [*shakes his head*]: . . . You?

ALLOTT: How do you sell an event that no one will admit is taking place?

PHILIPS: Have to go back to painting, old boy.

ALLOTT: I know when I'm licked, Philips. It's all or nothing . . . the avant-garde or bust.

PHILIPS: Old boy . . .

ALLOTT: It's not important.

PHILIPS: Don't give up . . . that's the message . . . that's the message that comes down to us from Rembrandt . . . from Cézanne . . . from all that countless host who sank their existences in art . . .

ALLOTT: Don't you get the feeling at times that it's a substitute for living?

PHILIPS: This *is* life . . . Dear boy . . . just look around you . . . the youth of today . . . the human body [*Indicates* STELLA.] . . . what more could one desire?

ALLOTT: You're right.

PHILIPS: How much do you want on?

ALLOTT: I haven't looked at a paper yet . . . I haven't got over the shock of this one . . . I even told my wife . . . on the phone, you know . . . we've been separated now for several months . . . '25p?' she said. 'You're going crazy.' And the fact of the matter is, at times, I really think I am.

PHILIPS: Baudelaire . . . Dostoevsky . . . Nietzsche . . . you have to bear them all in mind . . . men who teetered on the very brink of human existence and had the privilege – the temerity, even – to gaze right over the edge . . .

ALLOTT: I've gazed over the edge, Philips, long enough . . . it's the staying there that worries me . . . I'm beginning to think I'll never get back . . . How does one live as a revolutionary, Philips, when no one admits there's a revolution there?

PHILIPS: Prophet in his own country, old boy . . . Think of Christ.

ALLOTT: I think of nothing else . . . I'm even beginning to think, Philips, that it's not my duty to resurrect mankind.

PHILIPS: Stranger things have happened, boy . . . Lucky Horseshoe, two-fifteen . . . obvious choice . . . But then Blue Moon stuck out a mile.

ALLOTT: How much?

PHILIPS: Can get you eight to one, old boy.

ALLOTT [counting his money]: 10p . . . leaves me with 15.

PHILIPS: That's the spirit . . . [Takes the money.] Anything worth doing . . . [To CATHERINE as he leaves] Firmer! Firmer! . . . [To ALLOTT] Commit yourself: that's all it means. [Goes.

ALLOTT stands there for a while; gazes before him, abstracted. Then:]

ALLOTT: All right . . . Everyone?

BRENDA: Yes, sir.

CATHERINE: Yes, sir.

GILLIAN: Yes, sir.

MOONEY: Yes, sir.

WARREN: Yes, sir.

ALLOTT: Good . . .

MATHEWS: Yes, sir!

ALLOTT: Good . . . good. That's the spirit . . . Labor Ipse
Voluptas Est.

WARREN: Rest, sir?

ALLOTT: No, no . . . Just carry on.

[*Fade.*]

ACT TWO

Scene 1

Stage empty. Light faint.
> ABERCROMBIE *comes on, dressed in sweater, scarf, plimsolls,*
> *shorts. Carries a racquet.*
> *Silence.*
ABERCROMBIE: I say . . . [*Returns to screen: a moment later*
> *lights come on. Comes back.*] Anyone for squash?
> [*Groan from behind model's screen.*
> *Goes to screen: looks behind.*]
> I'm terribly sorry . . .
STELLA [*heard, stretching*]: Ooooh . . . !
ABERCROMBIE: Fancy a knock-up?
STELLA [*heard*]: No thanks.
ABERCROMBIE: Looks like thunder. [*Indicates off.*]
STELLA [*emerging in dressing-gown*]: I was sleeping . . .
> [*Stretches.*] It's so much quieter lying in here.
ABERCROMBIE [*ducking down and gazing up*]: Or snow . . .
STELLA: Play that often?
ABERCROMBIE: Lunch times . . . winter mostly. Summer
> – tennis.
STELLA: Oh . . . [*Stretches. Yawns.*] Make me feel so
> lazy . . . Got a cigarette?
> [ABERCROMBIE *takes cigarette packet from trouser-pocket.*]
> Give you one back . . . Left em in me knickers.
> [ABERCROMBIE *lights her cigarette with a lighter.*]
> Foley not around? [*Blows out smoke.*]
ABERCROMBIE: Doubt it.

STELLA: Been in his office have you?

ABERCROMBIE: Not very often.

STELLA: Seen his jars . . . ? *Bottles* . . . Along the shelves . . . Use them in chemistry labs, for acid.

ABERCROMBIE: Now you mention it.

STELLA: Full of urine.

ABERCROMBIE: What?

STELLA: Broke one, one day . . . cleaners. Terrible pong . . . His lavatory . . . would you believe, is full of broken statues . . . Venus de Milo in plaster-cast . . . all sorts of rubbish he's collected.

ABERCROMBIE: Good God.

STELLA: Keeps his pee in bottles: anything artistic – down the lav.

ABERCROMBIE: Good Lord.

STELLA: Suppose that's genius, really.

ABERCROMBIE: Yes . . .

STELLA: Modern art.

    [*Pause.*]

ABERCROMBIE: That's right. [*Looks around for* ALLOTT.]

STELLA: He was here not long ago . . . Mr Allott . . . Heard him singing.

ABERCROMBIE: Singing?

STELLA: He sings, you know, when he's on his own . . . Didn't know I was here, you see.

ABERCROMBIE: Ah, yes.

STELLA: What you use? [*Indicates racquet.*]

ABERCROMBIE: A rubber ball.

STELLA: I've always been interested, you know, in sport . . .

ABERCROMBIE: Ah, yes . . .

STELLA: My own colour, that. [*Reveals her shoulder.*]

ABERCROMBIE: Good lord.

STELLA: I've a greasy skin. Just feel at that.

ABERCROMBIE: It's very soft.

STELLA: A woman should be soft.

ABERCROMBIE: You've got very nice legs, of course.

STELLA: They're not so bad . . . woman my age. [*Shows him.*]

ABERCROMBIE: Don't know why you bother with that. [*Indicates dressing-gown.*]

STELLA: Can't sleep in me altogether. Not safe to in a place like this.

ABERCROMBIE: One or two custodians of morality about.

STELLA: Like who?

ABERCROMBIE: Me.

STELLA: Not from some of the tales I've heard.

ABERCROMBIE: Such as?

STELLA: Mr Abercrombie is a well-known character in some quarters of the town.

ABERCROMBIE: The tennis courts are the only place I frequent with any regularity . . . and the squash courts, too, of course.

[STELLA *turns back to the screen.*]

Room for two in there?

STELLA: There might.

ABERCROMBIE: Have a smoke, I think, myself . . . Give it up . . . [*Coughs.*] Chest . . . Never persist for very long.

STELLA: Sit, mind you. And nothing else.

[ABERCROMBIE *has gone behind the screen.*

STELLA *follows.*

After a moment ALLOTT *enters: slow. Takes hat off: sits down on edge of throne in his coat.*]

STELLA [*heard*]: Never . . . [*Laughter.*]

ABERCROMBIE [*heard*]: As God is my witness.

STELLA [*heard*]: All over?

ABERCROMBIE [*heard*]: That's what the genius said. [*Laughter, heard.*

ALLOTT *glances up: no interest: sits with arms on his*

knees. FOLEY *enters: stands there a moment, smoking pipe: takes it out.*]

FOLEY: Bloody place is like a mausoleum.

ALLOTT: Yes.

FOLEY: Lunch hour.

ALLOTT: Yes.

FOLEY: Chisel-marks on that wall out theer . . . Bring them up, you know, from the sculpture room: safe-keeping in their lockers. What they do? Start taking the bloody place apart. [*Gazes round: finally looks up. Reads:*]

  'Foley is never surely
  Going to keep us solely
  On potato crisps for long.'

Chalk.

ALLOTT: Yes.

FOLEY: Up yonder . . .

ALLOTT [*looks*]: Yes.

FOLEY: Know the author?

ALLOTT: No. [*Shakes his head.*]

 [*Pause.* FOLEY *looks round again. Pause.*]

FOLEY: Disillusioning place, is this.

ALLOTT: In what way?

FOLEY: Students of today . . . two minutes with a bucket of plaster . . . half a pot o' paint . . . a bit o' wire . . . turn out some conundrum on a piece of hardboard and think they've done a Mona Lisa. When you think this is where the Donatellos and the Verrocchios of the future are supposed to come from it begins to shake your faith.

 [*Sits down on the throne beside* ALLOTT.]

Ever think about life, then, do you?

ALLOTT [*hesitates for some considerable time. Then*]: No.

FOLEY: In my youth you thought of nothing else: life . . . [*Gazes up. Pause.*] Infinity . . . [*Pause. Abstracted. Then:*] Altered the pose, then, have you?

ALLOTT: I thought I'd bear it in mind . . . for a future occasion.

FOLEY: Classical, Allott. Classical. Every time. The distillation of history. The classical is the finest embodiment of the human spirit. That's what we're here to instil. A respect for the past and a clean and wholesome acceptance of the present . . . Vegetarian?

ALLOTT [looks up]: No.

FOLEY: Do you know what's involved in the killing of a cow?

ALLOTT [hesitates. Then]: No.

FOLEY: The dismemberment of a living body?

ALLOTT: No. [Shakes his head.]

FOLEY: I went to a butchery on one occasion . . . I don't call it by any of these fancy names . . . I went, ostensibly, to do some sketches – that's what I told the management – once there I found I couldn't draw a thing . . . Blood there was. Everywhere . . . intestines, bladders, stomachs, livers . . . the appalling desecration of life . . . the living reduced to an inanimate mass. [Pause.] Speak?

ALLOTT: No. [Shakes his head.]

FOLEY: I've never touched a piece of meat since then. Every time a piece of meat is presented to me at table . . . [Takes out penknife.] Cut my thumb.

ALLOTT [pause. Then]: Isn't it very dangerous?

FOLEY: I disinfect the blade . . . [Shows him blade.] Turns one or two stomachs, I can tell you that . . . I use it occasionally, too, for sharpening pencils. [Snaps blade to.] Not in the dining-room, I thought, today.

ALLOTT: No.

FOLEY: A consequence of illogical eating is illogical art. All good art is based on a good digestion. It's what these let-it-happen boys have never understood. Here today and gone tomorrow. They think abstraction, you know, can take art across national frontiers. Fact of the matter is, all the profoundest art is regional. It takes time for its universal principles to be revealed. For instance, who would have thought that a meticulous and obsessive interest in the Auvergne countryside would have made Cézanne one of the greatest – if not the greatest – painter of the present age. Draw a few rings, a few lines . . . blocks of colour, and because it's immediately recognizable in Tokyo, Lisbon and New York, think it must be significant . . . instant communication is the fallacy of the time. All these marvellous means for one human being to communicate with another – wireless, television, planes. What happens? Some terrible song-and-dance routine . . . beyond that: aeons of triviality perpetuating itself across the vast distances of interstellar space.

ALLOTT: I didn't eat because my wife has decided to divorce me, as a matter of fact.

FOLEY: Marriage for an artist is an anomaly in any case. When a man's life is illuminated by an inner vision, everything outside is pure distraction.

ALLOTT: That's her opinion exactly . . . [*Gets up.*] She thinks – with my working here – I'm neither one thing nor another . . . My creations – including, I would have thought, my marriage – invisible events which only I can see . . .

FOLEY [*rising*]: There's someone, you know, behind that screen. [*Goes over.*] Just look at this.

STELLA [*heard*]: Hello, Mr Foley.

FOLEY: Not been smoking by any chance, then, have you?

ABERCROMBIE [*heard*]: No, sir. [*Comes out stretching, glancing at* ALLOTT.] Fancy a shot or two, old man? [*Racquet.*]

ALLOTT: No, thanks.

FOLEY: Smell smoke, you know, a mile off. I've an

extremely sensitive nose for smoke. If somebody lights
up a cigarette a mile off I can smell it in a matter of
seconds.

ALLOTT [*gazing up, reading*]:
  'Some talk of Alexander and some of Hercules,
  But what of old Verrocchio and ancient Pericles?'
  [FOLEY *looks up too, and* ABERCROMBIE.]

FOLEY: How they get up there beats me . . . It takes
somebody more sophisticated than a student to think up
rhymes like that.

ALLOTT [*reading*]:
              'Teachers love to make a bit:
              All students do is shovel . . .'

FOLEY: It's not your casual two-minute composition
that . . . there's fifteen-minutes' worth of lettering on
that wall.

ALLOTT [*reads, in a fresh direction*]:
              'Allott is a parrot,
              Foley is a scream:
              Abercrombie's like a carrot,
              And Philips's just a queen.'

FOLEY: Get the whitewash in here this evening. You can't
turn your back on that. The Director of Education came
in the other day. Know what was inscribed in the front
doorway? 'Education is the opium of the middle classes.'
My father was a cobbler, and, before that, his father was
a blacksmith.

ABERCROMBIE: You've come a long way, Mr Foley.

FOLEY: I have . . . I have . . . I'll not have them forget it . . .
[*Sees* ABERCROMBIE *as if for the first time.*] You here for
the Monte Carlo Rally, are you?

ABERCROMBIE: Squash.

FOLEY: There's no squash in this building, I can tell you

that. Sport and art don't mix. What stimulates the brain stimulates the body: you don't need to go chasing balls to keep fit . . . We'll have that removed before I go tonight. [*Going: to* ALLOTT] Classical. Classical . . . It's the eternal, Allott, that really lasts. [*Goes.*

ALLOTT *sits down. He's still got on his coat. Pause.*

ABERCROMBIE *regards him for a moment. Then:*]

STELLA: I think I'll go for a pee. [*Goes.*]

ABERCROMBIE: True?

[ALLOTT *looks up.*]

Missis.

ALLOTT: My life has been a continual saga of good intentions, Abercrombie . . . I only became an artist because I thought that way I'd be of least trouble to anybody else . . . who's ever heard of an artist who's a liability?

ABERCROMBIE: Fancy a game or two, old man?

ALLOTT: Recline here, I think . . . Swot up on one or two classical poses . . . 'The Suicide's Revenge' . . . 'Love in Clover' . . . 'The Distinterested Man's Delight'.

ABERCROMBIE: Changeable situation . . . Might be back in time for bed.

ALLOTT: Not mine, I'm afraid. I'm sure of that.

ABERCROMBIE: Sure about the . . . ? [*Swings racquet.*

ALLOTT *nods.*]

ABERCROMBIE: See you.

ALLOTT: See you.

[ABERCROMBIE *goes.*

ALLOTT, *after a while, gets up: walks slowly round the stools. Finally sits down at one: gazes at the throne. Pause.*

After a little while MATHEWS *comes in, whistling.*]

MATHEWS: Sir. [*Nods.*

ALLOTT *nods.*]

MATHEWS: Mind? [*Indicates donkey.*]

ALLOTT: Not really.

MATHEWS: Stella . . . ? [*Nods at screen.*

  ALLOTT *shakes his head.*]

MATHEWS: Fancy a bit of that . . . You know . . . time to time. Not above it when you catch her on her own. Other people around: screams blue murder. [*Pause.*] Seen Foley . . .

ALLOTT: Yes.

MATHEWS: Tell you yesterday what happened?

ALLOTT: No . . .

MATHEWS: Came in . . . late . . . School as quiet as death . . . tip-toe up the stairs: look behind . . . *entering* the hall below is a very large piece of . . . can you guess?

  [ALLOTT, *after some moments' hesitation, shakes his head.*]

MATHEWS: Coal . . . [*Waits for* ALLOTT's *reaction.*] Two hands clasped to this gigantic piece of coal . . . big as a house . . . Know who it was? . . . Foley! . . . head comes in view . . . Looks this way . . . looks that . . . coal held out . . . looks up. Sees me. Know what he does? . . . Steps *backwards* . . . Couldn't believe it. Ever so slowly. After a few seconds this gigantic lump of coal just disappears . . . I go on up the stairs . . . Mark time. Steps get fainter . . . Two minutes later . . . piece of coal comes back . . . two hands . . . Foley . . . Tuck my head in . . . Steps out across the hall . . . Let him get half way . . . Call: '*Mr Foley, have you got a minute?*' . . . Should have seen it . . . crash like thunder . . . Look down . . . bits of coal all over the hall . . . Next thing: belting up the stairs and calling: '*Anybody smoking up here, then, is there?*' [*Laughs.*

  ALLOTT *no reaction.*

  Pause.]

Tell me he's a kleptomaniac.

ALLOTT: Is that so?

MATHEWS: Catch him one day.

ALLOTT: Sure to.

MATHEWS: Be in for the high-jump: can tell you that.

ALLOTT: There are plans, as a matter of fact, to replace this college with an Institute of Engineering . . . the designs are quite advanced, I understand . . . octagonal building with vertical lighting – no windows except in the roof – and a large gallery at one end for the mounting of exceptionally large pieces of machinery . . . what we want, in a nutshell, but it'll be given over exclusively to engines.

[MATHEWS *has mounted the throne.*]

MATHEWS: Fancied modelling, you know, myself . . . Do muscle exercises in the evening . . . [*Poses.*] . . . no threat of redundancy . . . alus somebody to look at somebody else.

ALLOTT: Yes.

[*Pause. He gazes at* MATHEWS.]

If you stand there for a moment . . . [*Takes out pad, pencil.*]

MATHEWS [*poses*]: This do you?

ALLOTT: Anything that comes natural.

[MATHEWS *poses.*

ALLOTT *draws casually. Silence.*]

MATHEWS: Strip down if you like.

ALLOTT: I think this'll do perfectly . . . you're posing very well.

MATHEWS: Think I'm loud-mouthed . . . [*Gestures off.*] Them . . . Fact is – do you mind me talking? – you act up to what people expect of you.

ALLOTT: How do you know what they expect?

MATHEWS: Feel it . . .

ALLOTT: Suppose you're mistaken?

MATHEWS: Not here.

ALLOTT: Suppose really they'd been expecting someone different?

MATHEWS: How different?

ALLOTT: Sensitive . . . intelligent . . . [*Still drawing.*] perhaps even quietly mannered.

MATHEWS: My looks?

ALLOTT: Looks can be deceptive.

MATHEWS: Long-distance only . . .

ALLOTT: Seen that wall?

MATHEWS: One o' your rhymes.

ALLOTT: Hardly.

MATHEWS: What?

ALLOTT: Not that tall.

MATHEWS [*reads*]: 'O where has the significance of life gone to . . .'

ALLOTT [*without looking up*]: 'My mother said.'

MATHEWS: '. . . If it's not where we might expect it, it must be in some other place instead.'

ALLOTT: Moving.

MATHEWS: Oh . . . Yeh. [*Adjusts his pose.*]

ALLOTT: That's better . . . No. No. That's fine. [*Draws in silence for a while.*

PHILIPS *comes in.*]

PHILIPS: Bet on . . . Odds as mentioned . . . [*Sees* MATHEWS.] Carter.

MATHEWS: Mathews.

PHILIPS: Mathews. [*Gazes at* MATHEWS *for some time.*]

MATHEWS [*finally, under* PHILIPS' *gaze*]: Mind if I get down, sir?

ALLOTT: One more minute.

MATHEWS: Arms ache.

ALLOTT: Ten seconds.

MATHEWS: Harder than you think.

PHILIPS: When I was in the pink could stand, utterly immobile, for an hour and a half . . . Reflex: a conditioned reflex. What's required, ironically enough, is to be utterly relaxed.

ALLOTT: Five.

PHILIPS: I've got the slip . . . Lucky Horseshoe.

ALLOTT: I'll never need it.

PHILIPS: Odds had shortened before I left. Sevens. It'll be three to one by the time they reach the post.

ALLOTT: Two.

MATHEWS: I'm going dizzy.

ALLOTT: Hold it. Hold it.

[MATHEWS, *after a strenuous effort to keep still, collapses.*
ALLOTT *goes on drawing for a moment.*
MATHEWS *sits moaning, massaging.*
ALLOTT *finally looks up: looks about him. Then:*]
Take this off . . . [*Coat: stands: removes it.*] Hang it. [*Feels in his pockets.*] Shan't be long. [*Goes.*]

MATHEWS: First time I've seen his drawing.

PHILIPS: One of the leading exponents of representational art in his youth, was Mr Allott . . . You'd have to go back to Michelangelo to find a suitable comparison . . .

[MATHEWS *stoops over pad: peers closely.*]

MATHEWS: There's nothing there . . .

PHILIPS: Now, of course . . . an impresario . . . purveyor of the invisible event . . . so far ahead of his time you never see it.

MATHEWS: I've been posing there for half an hour!

PHILIPS: Longer, I'd imagine.

MATHEWS [*picks up pad: examines other pages. Reads finally*]:
  'Oh, she was good all right in patches,
  She was good all right in bed:
  But where would it all have ended
  If I'd loved her like I said?'

PHILIPS: I really think that's private property, old boy.

MATHEWS [reads]:

> 'Oh, we'll listen to the wireless
> And lie in bed till three;
> "Turn up the volume, lady."
> Oh, love is good to me.'

[Evades PHILIPS' effort to take the pad.]

> 'Oh, he found love in valleys,
> In caves and crannies too;
> Fissures, where a lover
> Could find what lovers do.'

PHILIPS: I think, really, that belongs to me . . . is in my custody . . . my supervision.

MATHEWS [reads]:

> 'He called her night and morning;
> He sat beside the phone:
> What's mine is yours, she told him:
> Oh, give a dog a bone!'

PHILIPS: I'm appealing to you, Mathews, as a member of the staff . . . as a respected and somewhat elderly member of the staff . . . lightweight champion of the northern counties and – for several months previous to that – of one of the more prominent of the southern counties as well.

MATHEWS [reads]:

> 'He waited, how he waited;
> He waited for his love:
> She'd meant to get there early,
> But went back for her glove.'

PHILIPS: See here, Mathews . . . That's private property.

MATHEWS: Here . . . just look at this. [Shows it to PHILIPS.]

PHILIPS [reads]: 'I shall kill Foley . . . Foley is very poorly . . . Foley is surely . . . the person I shall hourly . . . kill . . . whenever poor old Allott gets the chance . . .'

MATHEWS: 'Poor old Allott is the . . .'

PHILIPS: 'Apotheosis . . .'

MATHEWS: 'Poor old Allott is the . . .'

PHILIPS: 'Amanuensis . . .'

MATHEWS: 'Poor old Allott is the . . .'

PHILIPS: 'Polarity . . .'

MATHEWS: 'From which this world began . . .'

PHILIPS: 'Poor old Al . . .'

MATHEWS: 'Poor old Allott . . .'

PHILIPS: 'Dirge on a forgotten planet . . .'

MATHEWS: 'Allott is the palette . . .'

PHILIPS: 'On which my sins began . . .'

MATHEWS: 'First . . .'

PHILIPS: 'He was a saviour . . .'

MATHEWS: 'Secondly . . .'

PHILIPS: 'A saint . . .'

MATHEWS: 'Thirdly . . .'

PHILIPS: 'Lost his chances . . .'

MATHEWS: 'Fourthly . . .'

PHILIPS: 'Learnt to paint.'

MATHEWS: 'Fifthly . . .'

PHILIPS: 'Came to pieces . . .'

MATHEWS: 'Sixthly . . .'

PHILIPS: 'Showed his hand.'

MATHEWS: 'Seventhly . . .'

PHILIPS: 'Set his creases . . .'

MATHEWS: 'Eighthly . . .'

PHILIPS: 'Joined the band.'

MATHEWS: 'Ninthly . . .'

PHILIPS: 'Went to heaven . . .'

MATHEWS: 'Tenthly . . .'

PHILIPS: 'Rang the bell.'

MATHEWS: 'Eleventhly . . .'
PHILIPS: 'Thought he'd better . . .'
MATHEWS: 'Twelfthly . . .'
ALLOTT [*having entered*]: 'Go to hell' . . . No, no, really, Philips . . . Once started, carry on . . .
PHILIPS: I was trying to get it from him. I was even – would you believe it – threatening him with physical violence.
MATHEWS: Private, sir. [*Hands it back.*] I was just looking at the drawing, sir.
ALLOTT: There isn't any drawing . . . or, rather, the drawing was the drawing . . . perhaps you weren't aware.
MATHEWS: No, sir. [*Pause. Then:*] I'll go and get my board, sir.
ALLOTT: Right.
  [MATHEWS *hesitates: glances from one to the other: goes.*]
PHILIPS [*examines watch*]: Better be getting back . . . Proceedings start in seven minutes . . . Six and a half to be exact . . . Carter moved the platform slightly.
ALLOTT: Mathews.
PHILIPS: Mathews . . . [*Adjusts it slightly.*] Right . . . [*Glances round.*] See you.
ALLOTT: See you.
  [PHILIPS *looks round once more: nods: goes.*
  ALLOTT *stays precisely where he is, standing.*
  Long pause.
  In the silence, eventually, STELLA *comes in.*]
STELLA: No one here?
ALLOTT: We're ready.
STELLA: Want me up?
ALLOTT: Pose.
  [STELLA *climbs on to the throne: disrobes. Stands there. Then:*]
STELLA: How do you want me?
ALLOTT: Natural.

[STELLA *poses.*]

STELLA: Where are the others?

ALLOTT: Coming.

[SAUNDERS *enters. Moves round self-consciously in duffle-coat, board beneath his arm: considers which of the donkeys he might take.*]

SAUNDERS: Snowing.

ALLOTT: Really?

SAUNDERS: Outside . . . Stella.

STELLA: Hello, Samuel.

SAUNDERS: The name's Terry. Samuel or Sammy is a nickname given me by the students.

STELLA: I'm sorry, Terry.

SAUNDERS: Do you mind if I sit here?

STELLA: Keep an eye on you.

SAUNDERS: I prefer to see your face . . . I don't like human beings to be set down as objects . . . Are you drawing as well, Mr Allott?

ALLOTT: I . . . create, Saunders, in an altogether different dimension.

[SAUNDERS *settles himself. Pause. Then:*]

SAUNDERS: The human condition . . . is made up of many ambivalent conditions . . . that's one thing I've discovered . . . love, hatred . . . despair, hope . . . exhilaration, anguish . . . and it's not these conditions themselves that are of any significance but the fact that, as human beings, we oscillate between them . . . It's the oscillation between hope and despair that's the great future of our existence, not the hope, or the despair, in themselves.

[*Pause.*]

STELLA: It's a wonderful observation . . .

[*Pause.* SAUNDERS *settles himself: gets out his equipment.*]

I like people who think about life.

SAUNDERS: I don't think about life. I'm merely interested in recording it.

STELLA: I see.

[SAUNDERS *sets up his plumb-line and strings, etc., facing* STELLA.]

SAUNDERS: I think Mr Allott is quite correct: all great art is truly impersonal. All great *lives* are impersonal . . . To live truly you have to be . . .

ALLOTT: Impersonal.

SAUNDERS: It's only the disinterested person who sees what's truly there. I learnt that from you, sir.

ALLOTT: Yes.

SAUNDERS: These others have no regard for anything . . . They have no *conception* of those qualities which can lift a man above his habitual animal existence.

ALLOTT: No.

SAUNDERS: Can you lift your head a bit higher, Stella . . .

STELLA: Like this?

SAUNDERS [*examines her for a while in silence. Then*]: Yes.

[*Roar outside*: MATHEWS, WARREN, MOONEY, GILLIAN, BRENDA *and* CATHERINE *enter in a noisy group*. WARREN: 'All over the bloody floor!' *Laughter*.]

GILLIAN: We've started.

ALLOTT: To your donkeys, men . . .

[MATHEWS *blows raspberry. Laughter*.]

CATHERINE: Sir! It's a new one.

BRENDA: The light's all different.

ALLOTT: Sufficient unto the day is the evil thereof, Catherine.

CATHERINE: Sir! I've got to start all over again . . . !

WARREN: Improvise.

ALLOTT: Improvisation is the hallmark of the bereft imagination . . . Draw, Catherine . . . Brenda . . . Warren . . . Carter . . . Mathews . . . Mooney . . . Gillian . . . Draw.

Register, merely, what you see before you.

[MATHEWS *blows raspberry: laughter.*]

WARREN [*calling*]: How are you, Sammy?

SAUNDERS: All right.

BRENDA: Brought your binoculars, have you?

MATHEWS: Now, then. Now, then. What have we got here? [*Rubs hands, gazes at* STELLA, *standing over his donkey.*] Head, hands, feet, two tits . . . a pair o' smashers . . . all correct and ready to go. [*Salutes: raspberry: gets down to it.*

Silence slowly descends: WARREN *belches: laughter.*

Silence descends again. Then:]

BRENDA: Quiet, i'n it?

[*Laughter. Silence grows again: snigger – muffled; titter – muffled.*

Long pause.]

Whatch'a have, then?

GILLIAN: Sago.

WARREN: Terrible.

MATHEWS: Never eat here.

CARTER: Go to the Excelsior myself.

CATHERINE: That restaurant?

CARTER: Snack-bar . . . soup, coffee: that's all you need for lunch.

WARREN [*belches*]: To the pub, personally, myself.

MOONEY: Can't afford it.

MATHEWS: Catering for two.

MOONEY: Piss off.

[WARREN *belches.*

They go on drawing.

ALLOTT *stands at the back: abstracted.*

Silence.]

GILLIAN: You've got a spot, Stella.

STELLA: Where?

GILLIAN: Left leg.

CARTER: Look at it *later*.

CATHERINE: Inside your knee.

STELLA: Oh . . . yes!

BRENDA: I've got some ointment.

CARTER: Later.

WARREN: Later!

CATHERINE: Honestly!

> [STELLA *gazes at them: resumes her pose.*
> *Silence. Then:*]

MATHEWS: What you drawing, Gillian?

GILLIAN: Not you.

MOONEY: Leave her alone, fart-face.

MATHEWS [*to* MOONEY: *makes a fist*]: Push this up your nose.

MOONEY: Push it up somewhere else might be more useful.

MATHEWS: Look! [*Rises threateningly.*]

ALLOTT [*stepping forward*]: I thought – with your permission – I might pose myself.

CATHERINE: Sir!

BRENDA: Sir.

CATHERINE: How super!

GILLIAN: Not in the nude, sir!

ALLOTT: Why not?

CATHERINE: Oh . . . sir!

WARREN: Go on, sir . . . Let 'em have it!

ALLOTT: I thought it might be an inducement . . .

BRENDA: Sir!

ALLOTT: The sort, Brenda, of whose absence you were complaining only a little while ago.

CATHERINE: Sir! You can't.

MATHEWS: Here . . . go on, sir. I'll come up with you!

> [MATHEWS *springs up on to the throne:*

screams: roars of laughter.

STELLA *descends, screaming: snatches her dressing-gown.*
The girls laugh: WARREN *shouts encouragement:* 'Go on!']
Five–minute poses. Who's gonna keep the time?

BRENDA: Stop him, sir. Stop him.

[MATHEWS *has begun to remove his clothes.*]

WARREN: Get it out then, Matty! Get it out!

MATHEWS: Who'll join me, then! Who'll join me!

[*Laughter: jeers.*]

SAUNDERS: It's the dividing line, you see, between life and
art . . . Stella represents it in its impersonal condition . . .
Mathews represents its . . .

WARREN: Get your prick out . . . ! Here . . . here, then. Go
on. Grab her.

[*Has already risen: seizes* STELLA *and forces her back,*
struggling, to the throne.
Laughter.]

MATHEWS: Here, come on, let's have a hold as well!

[*They struggle with the screaming* STELLA *between them.*]

CATHERINE: Sir . . . ! Stop him, sir!

WARREN: Go on, then . . . Get it out, then, Mathews . . .
get it in.

MATHEWS: I can't . . . I can't . . .

[*Laughter.*]

WARREN: Lie still, for God's sake . . .

STELLA: Get off . . . [*Screaming.*] Get off!

WARREN: Get it in, for God's sake.

MATHEWS: I am. I am.

STELLA: Get off . . . Get off . . . Get him off.

WARREN: Go on: thump it. Thump it.

MATHEWS: I am! . . . I am! [*Still struggling to straddle* STELLA.
STELLA *laughs, half-screams at* MATHEWS' *efforts.*

ALLOTT *stands, pausing, halfway between the donkeys and the throne.*

SAUNDERS *gazes transfixed.*

CARTER *calls out encouragement, laughing.*

GILLIAN *gazes, blank, uncomprehending.*

MOONEY *has stepped forward as if he might intervene.*

BRENDA's *got up: crossed halfway and stays there.*

CATHERINE *stays sitting, her pen still in her hand.*]

WARREN: Get it in . . . Get it in . . . thump it, Mathews . . . thump it . . .

MATHEWS: Hold her! Hold her!

STELLA: Get off . . . Get him off.

WARREN: Get your legs open, Stella.

STELLA: Get him off.

WARREN: Get it in, for God's sake.

STELLA: No . . . No . . .

MATHEWS: I am! . . . I am! . . . Oh God . . . Here! . . . It's lovely.

CATHERINE: Sir! Sir!

WARREN: Thump it!

MATHEWS: *I am! I am!*

BRENDA: Sir . . . For God's sake, sir . . .

CATHERINE: Fetch Mr Foley!

WARREN: Thump it! Thump it . . . Go on, Matt . . . Here. Come on . . . let's have a go!

GILLIAN: Sir! Tell him to stop it. Sir! . . . Tell him!

WARREN: Here . . . here . . . Come on. Let's have it!

MATHEWS: I'm coming . . . I'm coming! . . . God . . . Oh God . . . I'm coming . . . ! Hold her . . . Hold her.

STELLA: No . . . *No!*

CATHERINE: Sir! Sir! For God's sake, sir!

MATHEWS: Oh! [*Falls, moaning, over her. Moans: his movements slow. Slows: stillness.*]

WARREN: Jesus . . . Look . . . He has, an' all . . . Bloody

hell. Didn't think he had it in him. Cor blimey, Mathews . . . [*Laughs.*

CATHERINE *sits dumbfounded.*

GILLIAN *has covered her face with her hands.*]

MOONEY: Jesus . . . [*Turns to* CARTER.]

CARTER: *The dirty bugger.*

MOONEY: *The dirty sod.*

[SAUNDERS *still sits there, dazed.*

CARTER *hasn't moved.*

WARREN *stands by the throne, contemplating* MATHEWS, *seemingly incredulous: stoops over* STELLA *finally.*]

WARREN: You all right, Stell?

[BRENDA *still sits there, gazing at* STELLA.

MATHEWS, *bowed, raises his head: gazes at the others: smiles; then, straightening, he breaks into laughter.*

WARREN *breaks into laughter: dances down from platform.*] Had you! Had you . . . ! Thought he had . . . ! [*Dances in front of* BRENDA, CATHERINE.

MATHEWS *sits, cross-legged on the platform, laughing.*] Thought he'd had her, didn't you, love!

BRENDA: You dirty filthy beast. Disgusting . . . [*To* ALLOTT] It's disgusting, sir.

WARREN: She thought you'd had it in there, Mathews. [*To* BRENDA] Give us something to go home with, love.

CATHERINE: How could you! Let him do it, sir!

WARREN: Had her going. Didn't we, love!

BRENDA: Piss off.

MATHEWS: Stick of dynamite. [*Flourishes himself: fanfare.*

WARREN *and* MATHEWS *laugh.*]

ALLOTT: If you wouldn't mind . . . Stella . . . [*Invites her to resume her pose.*]

WARREN [*to* STELLA]: Lit her fuse then, have we, love?

STELLA: Get off!

GILLIAN: I think it was obscene, vulgar and disgusting.

WARREN: It's the on'y three words she bloody knows.

CATHERINE: Why did you let him do it, sir? Why did you start him off?

[ALLOTT *gazes at them.*

MATHEWS *has climbed down from the throne, straightening his clothes, laughing.*]

ALLOTT: My own effort was to have been altogether less sensational . . . That's to say, dispassionate . . . [*Quieter*] . . . I would have posed for you quite gladly . . . as it is . . .

CATHERINE: Here . . . are you all right, sir?

ALLOTT: The essence of any event, Catherine . . . is that it should be . . . indefinable. Such is the nature . . . the ambivalence — as Saunders so aptly described it — of all human responses . . . love, hate . . . anguish . . . hope? Was it hope you made a corollary of anguish . . . ? Far be it from me to intrude . . . my domestic circumstance . . . my personal life is my own affair . . . can play no part in what, to all intents and purposes, may well be happening here . . . a personal element which, despite all my efforts, I cannot . . . understandably . . . restrain . . . thorn within the flesh . . . The prospect of presenting myself to you, even now, in what may be described as a human condition isn't all that repellent to me . . . It's merely that . . . it would no longer be, as it were, a work of art . . . merely . . . another aspect of a human being. [*Pause. Then:*] I suppose the best solution . . . Warren . . . Mathews . . . is to return to the job in hand . . . I to instruct; you to be instructed . . . Stella.

[STELLA *looks round:*

MATHEWS *and* WARREN *have returned to their donkeys: silence.*

ALLOTT *straightens the throne: positions and straightens the white cloth: pauses: waits.*

227

STELLA, *after a moment's hesitation, climbs up: glances at the students: disrobes: takes up her pose.*

Then, in the silence:]

SAUNDERS: Head to the left, Stella . . . Arm . . .

[STELLA *follows* SAUNDERS' *instructions.*]

That's right.

ALLOTT: If you'd resume your various . . . and singularly varied . . .

[*Pause.*

They begin to draw.]

No work of art is complete without a personal statement. After all, the tradition we're ostensibly working in here is one which declares art to be a residual occupation . . . that is to say, it leaves objects – certain elements of its activity – behind . . . stone, paint, canvas . . . bronze . . . paper . . . carbon . . . a synthesis of natural elements convened by man . . . whereas we, elements as it were of a work ourselves, partake of existence . . . simply by being what we are . . . expressions of a certain time and place, and class . . . defying . . . hope . . . defying anguish . . . defying, even, definition . . . more substantial than reality . . . stranger than a dream . . . figures in a landscape . . . scratching . . . scraping . . . rubbing . . . All around us . . . our rocky ball . . . hurtling through time . . . Singing . . . to no one's tune at all.

[*Fade.*

Dark.]

Scene 2

Light comes up: as before: throne, donkeys, heaters, easels,
screens: empty. After a while BRENDA *comes in: coat on, canvas*
bag.

BRENDA: Gone.

    [CATHERINE *enters: coat, cap, bag.*]

CATHERINE: No use waiting.

BRENDA: Hang on.

    [*She goes to upstage screen:*
    SAUNDERS *enters: coat on, scarf.*]

SAUNDERS: Hey: what're you doing?

BRENDA: Piss off.

    [BRENDA *brings out* STELLA's *bags from behind the screen.*]

CATHERINE: Has Mr Allott gone?

SAUNDERS: He's in Foley's office.

BRENDA: You report it, Sammy? [*Hands one of the bags to*
    CATHERINE.]

SAUNDERS: Somebody's got to be responsible for decency
    and order.

CATHERINE: Lose his job, I shouldn't wonder.

BRENDA: Pity somebody, Saunders, didn't lose something
    else.

SAUNDERS: Allott's trouble is that he's got no discipline.
    He lets his theories run away with him. Art and life, in
    that respect, are separate things. No one should allow
    life to monopolize art: and similarly no one should allow
    art to be engulfed by life.

BRENDA: You in charge in here?

    [SAUNDERS *has begun to straighten the donkeys: takes*
    white sheet from the throne: begins to fold it.]

SAUNDERS: It would have been reported in any case. I'm

not averse to taking on that responsibility. Somebody has to do it. Even if it puts them in bad odour with everybody else . . . They'll need this place, in any case, tomorrow.

CATHERINE: What for?

BRENDA: Another orgy.

SAUNDERS: To create something out of chaos, Catherine . . . To invigorate. Distil. Not to deprave. To illuminate. Art, Catherine, should be an example. Not a reflection. If life itself is degenerate then art should set ideals.

BRENDA: He *is* taking over. [*To* CATHERINE] Got your hat?

[ALLOTT *enters: coat over arm, hat and gloves in hand.*
Pause.

They wait: SAUNDERS *goes on tidying up.*]

ALLOTT: What are you doing with that?

CATHERINE: They're Stella's, sir.

ALLOTT: She's quite capable of collecting them herself.

BRENDA: She didn't want to come up, sir.

ALLOTT: She's got two arms, two legs; there's nothing to prevent her.

CATHERINE: We thought it'd be kinder to take them down.

ALLOTT: I think, on the whole, it might be kinder to leave them here.

[*They hesitate: glance at each other: put the bags down.*]

BRENDA: We came up to say goodnight, sir.

ALLOTT: Goodnight.

[*Pause:* CATHERINE *and* BRENDA *look at one another.*
Then:]

CATHERINE: Goodnight, then, sir.

[*They go.*

SAUNDERS *works, tidying.*

ALLOTT *watches a moment. Then:*]

230

ALLOTT: I have to thank you, evidently . . . for taking the part of public decency and order in this matter, Saunders.

SAUNDERS: That's right.

ALLOTT: I thought, on the whole, you enjoyed it. Gave you something to speculate about . . . All the artist needs, after all, is *meat* – something to react to, report on, comment about, differentiate between . . . *record* . . . he never has to act. At least, that's how I've always understood it.

SAUNDERS: Perhaps we're talking, sir, about a different kind of art.

ALLOTT: Evidently. I've lost my job.

SAUNDERS: I'm sorry to hear that, sir.

ALLOTT: So am I. I've lost a wife . . . I've also lost my sole means, if it were at all desirable, of supporting her. It seems I'll have to dig deeper into my already somewhat limited resources and find what other potentialities might be lying there . . . as a revolutionary and a leader of the avant-garde – purveyor of the invisible event, marching ahead of my time – it seems my already overtaxed imagination has not been taxed enough.

SAUNDERS [*looking round*]: If there's nothing else, I'll go.

ALLOTT: That's very kind.

[*The room is tidy: pause.*]

SAUNDERS: Goodnight, then, sir.

ALLOTT: Goodnight.

[SAUNDERS *goes to the exit. Then:*]

SAUNDERS: If you should ever feel the need to discuss why I acted like I did I'll always be available, sir.

ALLOTT: You better go, Saunders . . . Your kindness . . . positively . . . overwhelms me. Any further display of it will reduce me – I can assure you, Saunders – to something very little short of tears.

SAUNDERS: Goodnight, then, sir. [*Goes.*

ALLOTT *stands there a moment: stiff, expectant.* CARTER *enters.*]

CARTER: I'm off, sir.

ALLOTT [*looks up*]: Right.

CARTER: Sorry to hear about your difference with the Principal, sir.

ALLOTT: Scarcely a difference, Carter.

CARTER: No, sir.

ALLOTT: More in the nature I would have thought of a final solution.

CARTER: Anything I can do, sir?

ALLOTT [*looks round: donkeys in a neat row: throne straight, sheet folded*]: It seems everything's been done.

CARTER [*hesitates. Then*]: Goodnight, then, sir.

ALLOTT: Goodnight, Carter.

[CARTER *nods, hesitates, then goes: laughter, whistling, cries, jeers off.*

WARREN *enters, followed a moment later by* MATHEWS: *evidently they've been tussling with* CARTER, *off.*]

WARREN: Night, sir!

ALLOTT: Night, Warren.

MATHEWS: Just popped in, sir. Say cheerio.

ALLOTT: Cheerio.

WARREN: Sorry to hear the news, sir.

ALLOTT: That's right.

MATHEWS: Any time you want a reference, sir.

ALLOTT: I'll not forget.

WARREN: You're the tops for us, sir.

MATHEWS: Every time!

[*Laughter: horse with each other.*]

WARREN: Night, sir.

MATHEWS: Night, sir.

ALLOTT: Goodnight.

[*They go: pass* PHILIPS *entering:*

'Night, Mr Philips!'

'Night, Mr Philips, sir!' *Laughter.*

PHILIPS *is wrapped up: coat, cap, scarf.*]

PHILIPS: Sevens, old boy! [*Thumbs up.*]

ALLOTT: Snow, of course, could easily postpone it.

PHILIPS: Snow, old boy: hadn't thought of that . . . Still. [*Claps gloved hands.*] Ours not to reason.

ALLOTT: No, old man.

PHILIPS: Well . . . See you, Allott.

ALLOTT: See you.

PHILIPS [*hesitates. Then*]: Goodnight. [*Goes.*

ALLOTT *looks round: one last donkey marginally out of line: carefully adjusts it: lines it up exactly: squints along it: adjusts it once again. Readjusts.*

Then: ABERCROMBIE *enters: wrapped up, no bowler hat.*]

ABERCROMBIE: Seen Foley?

ALLOTT: Some rearrangement of the curriculum, it appears, is being considered . . . as the result of certain unedifying scenes observed by at least one member of the student body . . . as a consequence of which a somewhat more traditional form of life-class may well be introduced . . . Revolution, after all, is not a self-perpetuating process . . . it does, by definition, they tell me, come to an end.

ABERCROMBIE: That's right.

ALLOTT: I've always seen myself as something of a pil-grim . . . a goal so mystical it defies description . . . not gates, exactly, I see before me . . . more nearly, Aber-crombie . . . [*Gazes directly at him.*] a pair of eyes. [*Pause. Examines* ABERCROMBIE. *Then:*] I attempted to nego-tiate . . . true instinct of the employee . . . scenes of rape . . . masturbatory tendencies evident amongst my pupils which I made no attempt to discourage – if anything, according to reports, I did everything to stimulate . . . bartering silence over *my* chef d'oeuvre if I gave to the authorities no information about our Principal's own cloacal masterpiece – toilet seat a pedestal for one of the more lyrical outpourings of Praxiteles . . . Decency in the end, Abercrombie, you'll be pleased to hear, prevailed. Mr Foley is cleaning up his toilet – leaving no evidence, as it were, behind. No artist, after all, I decided, should condemn another . . . We are all, I've come to realize, *brothers* . . . even if some, it transpires, have to be more brotherly than others . . . Michelangelo's David and Caravaggio's Disciples at Emmaus – to name but two – were not that easily come by: they were the process of a great deal of mental pain. I shall let that anguish, Abercrombie, go before me . . . Go before me and – if the past is anything to go by – light my way.

[MOONEY *enters, followed by* GILLIAN *holding his hand.*]
MOONEY: I came to say goodnight, sir.
ALLOTT: Goodnight, Mooney . . . Goodnight, Gillian.
[MOONEY *waits for* GILLIAN *to answer.*]
GILLIAN: All I wanted to say, sir.
ALLOTT: Yes?
GILLIAN: I don't hold you to blame, sir.
ALLOTT: That's very commendable.
GILLIAN: It's the circumstances, sir.
ALLOTT: That's quite correct . . . But then, in a way, Gillian, I created them. That, after all, is my modus operandi . . . preparation . . . assembly . . . pound, grind, mix . . . colour sublimated somewhat by the immediate surround . . . partaking nevertheless – to some extent – of our . . . relatively, Gillian . . . unadulterated human temperament . . . yours, and yours . . . and . . . [*Pauses: indicates* ABERCROMBIE.] his . . . My next work may be something altogether less commendable . . . That's to say, more . . . substantial . . . if not altogether

234

more extravagant than what I appeared to have achieved today . . . I shall have to see . . . sans means . . . sans wife . . . sans recognition who's to know what I . . . might rise to . . .

[*Pause. Then:*]

MOONEY: We wish you luck, sir.

ALLOTT: Thank you, Mooney.

GILLIAN: Goodnight, then, sir.

ALLOTT: Goodnight, Gillian.

[*They hesitate: glance at* ALLOTT *once more: nod, then go.*]

ABERCROMBIE: I suppose I better go as well . . . Anything I can do?

ALLOTT: Ahead of its time . . . impossible to perceive . . . the pageant is at an end now, Abercrombie . . . The process, as you can see, is virtually complete.

[ABERCROMBIE *gazes around him. Then:*]

ABERCROMBIE: See you, sport.

ALLOTT: See you.

[ABERCROMBIE *nods, smiles, and goes.*
ALLOTT *pauses: sits.*
Silence.
After a while STELLA *enters: dressed for the cold: coat, scarf, gloves, beret. Nods at* ALLOTT: *goes to screen.*]

If you're looking for these, I've got them here.

STELLA: Said they'd brought them down. Looked all over.

ALLOTT: Recovered, have you?

STELLA: Think so. [*Tucking her hair beneath her beret, ready to leave.*]

ALLOTT: Violation, they tell me, is a prerequisite of art . . . disruption of prevailing values . . . re-integration in another form entirely. What you see and feel becomes eternal . . . a flower grows . . . a million million years it takes to blossom . . . [*Waits.*] Will you be coming up tomorrow?

STELLA: I suppose so . . . [*Checks bags.*] Shopping . . .
[*Examines contents.*] . . . [*Looks up.*] See you, Mr Allott.

ALLOTT: See you.

[*As* STELLA *goes*]:
Would you . . .
[*She pauses, turning*]:
. . . put out the light?
[*Pauses: nods: she goes: a moment later the light diminishes.*
ALLOTT *stands: pulls on his coat: puts on his hat.*
FOLEY *enters in the half-light.*]

FOLEY: Still here, are you.
[*Pause: he gazes round.*]

ALLOTT: That's right.
[FOLEY *gazes overhead for a while. Then:*]

FOLEY: Thought of writing one up myself. [*Nods at wall.*]
'When is a man not a man?' [*Pause.*] I could never think
of a second line.

ALLOTT: That's right.

FOLEY: It's not without some regret . . . [*Gestures to him.*]
You leaving.

ALLOTT: No.

FOLEY: I hope you'll find your next appointment more
rewarding.

ALLOTT: I don't know . . . It's had its compensations,
Principal . . . I've achieved some of my best work, I
think, in here.

FOLEY: I believe in forgiveness, Allott . . . Apart from a
good digestion, it's the one indispensable principle of
human growth.

ALLOTT: That's right.

FOLEY: A man – if he puts his mind to it – can always mend
his ways. Experience, you see, can put you right . . . In
here, the mind atrophies, hardens: when the soul is
constipated it means the nourishment isn't right.

ALLOTT: I'll keep my bowels open.

FOLEY: It'll make a difference, I can tell you that . . . You'll leave the life-room tidy? [*Waits for* ALLOTT's *acknowledgement.*] Set an example, otherwise no one follows. [*Puts out his hand.*] I better say goodnight.

ALLOTT: Goodnight, Principal. [*Shakes his hand.*

FOLEY *looks round, briskly: nods: he goes.*

ALLOTT *looks round: draws on his gloves: pulls up his collar: looks round once again, freshly: goes.*

Fade.]

MORE ABOUT PENGUINS
AND PELICANS

For further information about books available from Penguins please write to Dept EP, Penguin Books Ltd, Harmondsworth, Middlesex UB7 0DA.

In the U.S.A.: For a complete list of books available from Penguins in the United States write to Dept CS, Penguin Books, 625 Madison Avenue, New York, New York 10022.

In Canada: For a complete list of books available from Penguins in Canada write to Penguin Books Canada Ltd, 2801 John Street, Markham, Ontario L3R 1B4.

In Australia: For a complete list of books available from Penguins in Australia write to the Marketing Department, Penguin Books Australia Ltd, P.O. Box 257, Ringwood, Victoria 3134.